PEARSON Chemistry

Chemistry Skills and Math Workbook

PEARSON

Boston, Massachusetts • Chandler, Arizona • Glenview, Illinois • Upper Saddle River, New Jersey

ISBN-13: 978-0-13-320449-0
ISBN-10: 0-13-320449-X

PEARSON

ISBN-13:   978-0-13-320449-0
ISBN-10:   0-13-320449-9

6   16

CONTENTS

Interpret Graphs Plastic Packaging in Waste   Lesson 1.2

Preview the Graph

Study the bar graph. The graph presents
data on the amount of plastic packaging in
U.S. waste. Plastic packaging includes
items such as water bottles and milk jugs.
Waste includes items that end up in landfills
and items that are recycled.

Year is the variable on the *x*-axis. For what
years are data given?

_____

_____

The variable on the *y*-axis is waste produced. What is the unit for waste produced?

_____

To change a value from thousands of tons to tons, you can multiply the value by 1000.
How many tons are in 2500 thousands of tons?

_____

Analyze the Graph

Now you are ready to answer some more questions. As you read the questions:

▶ Highlight key words.

▶ Circle numbers and units.

Use the first question as an example.

1. **Read Graphs** How many thousands of tons of plastic
   packaging were in U.S. waste in 1960? How many tons of
   plastic packaging were in the waste?

   _____

   _____

   > Try it! Find the bar for
   > 1960. Read the value at the
   > top of the bar. Multiply the
   > answer by 1000 to find the
   > number of tons.

2. **Calculate** How did the number of tons of plastic packaging in
   U.S. waste change between 1960 and 1970?

   _____

   _____

   > Try it! Subtract the value
   > for 1960 from the value for
   > 1970. Then multiply the
   > answer by 1000.

3. Compare In which decade was the increase in plastic packaging waste greater: between 1960 and 1970 or between 1970 and 1980?

_____

_____

> Try it! Compare the heights of the bars for 1960 and 1970. Then compare the heights of the bars for 1970 and 1980.

4. Estimate In what year was the amount of plastic packaging waste about double what it was in 1990?

_____

_____

> Try it! Find the value in thousands of tons for 1990. Then find the bar with a value that is about twice that value.

On Your Own

5. Read Graphs How many tons of plastic packaging were in U.S. waste in 2007?

_____

6. Calculate How did the number of tons of plastic packaging in U.S. waste change between 1960 and 2007?

_____

7. Calculate About how many times more U.S. plastic packaging waste was there in 1990 than in 1980?

_____

8. Make Generalizations Describe the pattern shown in the graph for plastic packaging waste between 1960 and 2007.

_____

_____

9. Predict Will the amount of plastic packaging in U.S. waste increase or decrease in the next 10 years? Explain.

_____

_____

_____

1 Standardized Test Prep Tutor

Read the question. The key phrase in the question stem has a blue highlight.

2. An analytical chemist is most likely to
   - (A) explain why paint is stirred before it is used.
   - (B) explain what keeps paint attached to the steel frame of an automobile.
   - (C) identify the type of paint chips found at the scene of a hit-and-run accident.
   - (D) investigate the effect of leaded paint on the development of a young child.

❶ **Analyze**

An analytical chemist studies what matter is made of. Each answer describes a possible scientific study. Look for a study that involves the composition of a material.

❷ **Solve**

Look at the answer choices one at a time.

In answer A, the study is about the properties of paint.

In answer B, the study is about what keeps paint attached to a metal. So the focus is on the interactions between two known materials.

In answer C, the study is about the type of paint chips found at a crime scene. To identify the chips, the chemist needs to identify the compounds in the paint.

In answer D, the substance being studied is known. What is not known is how lead affects the growth of a child.

❸ **Choose an Answer**

Which answer choice involves the study of what matter is made of? The correct answer is C.

Now you try it.

An organic chemist is most likely to
- (A) study a reaction between hydrogen and oxygen.
- (B) develop new carbon-based fuels.
- (C) explain how a firefly produces flashes of light.
- (D) identify the other metals in a gold necklace.

Use this paragraph to answer Questions 8–10. You will be shown how to solve Questions 8 and 9, and then you will solve Question 10 on your own.

(A) One day, your car does not start. (B) You say, "The battery is dead!" (C) Your friend uses a battery tester and finds that the battery has a full charge. (D) Your friend sees corrosion on the battery terminals. (E) Your friend says, "Maybe corrosion is causing a bad connection in the electrical circuit, preventing the car from starting." (F) Your friend cleans the terminals, and the car starts.

8. Which statements are observations?

9. Which statements are hypotheses?

10. Which statements describe experiments?

Read the paragraph once before you try to answer the questions. Each sentence in the paragraph is a statement and each statement has a letter label. After you finish reading, focus on one question at a time.

8. Which statements are observations?

An observation is information you obtain by using your senses—sight, sound, hearing, touch, and taste.

Find the statements in the paragraph that describe observations.

Statement A is an observation because you would have heard sounds or felt vibrations if the engine had started. Statement D is an observation because your friend *sees* corrosion on the battery terminals.

The use of the plural "statements" in the question suggests that the paragraph contains more than one observation.

9. Which statements are hypotheses?

A hypothesis is a proposed explanation for an observation. Look for statements in the paragraph that offer an explanation for the observations you identified in Question 8.

Statement B is a hypothesis because it explains why the car did not start. Statement E is a hypothesis because it explains why rust on the battery terminals could keep the car from starting.

Now you try it.

10. Which statements describe experiments?

Hint: Think about the definition of an experiment and look for statements that match the definition.

_____

_____

Interpret Data Comparing Physical Properties

Lesson 2.1

Preview the Table

The table has five columns. The column on the left lists the names of twelve substances. The rest of the columns list physical properties of each substance. What are the physical properties listed in the table?

_____

_____

Look at the column that lists the state of each substance at room temperature. How many substances listed in the table are gases at room temperature?

_____

Physical Properties of Some Substances				
Substance	State	Color	Melting point (°C)	Boiling point (°C)
Neon	Gas	Colorless	−249	−246
Oxygen	Gas	Colorless	−218	−183
Chlorine	Gas	Greenish-yellow	−101	−34
Ethanol	Liquid	Colorless	−117	78
Mercury	Liquid	Silvery-white	−39	357
Bromine	Liquid	Reddish-brown	−7	59
Water	Liquid	Colorless	0	100
Sulfur	Solid	Yellow	115	445
Aluminum	Solid	Silver	660	2519
Sodium chloride	Solid	White	801	1413
Gold	Solid	Yellow	1064	2856
Copper	Solid	Reddish-yellow	1084	2562

Look at the column that lists the color of substances. Which substances in the table are colorless?

_____

Look at the columns that list the melting point and boiling point of each substance. What units are used for melting point and boiling point?

_____

Analyze the Table

Now you are ready to answer some more questions. As you read the questions:

► Highlight key words.
► Circle numbers and units.

Use the first question as an example.

1. **Identify** Which substance in the table has the highest melting point? Which substance has the lowest melting point?

   Highest melting point = _____

   Lowest melting point = _____

> **Try it!** Look at the melting point column. Find the highest or lowest value. Move your finger to the left across the row to find the substance with that value.

2. Compare Which physical properties are shared by sulfur and gold?

_____

_____

Try it! Look at the physical properties of sulfur and gold. Write down the properties that are the same for both substances.

On Your Own

3. Identify Which colorless substance boils at 78°C?

_____

4. Read Tables What are the physical properties of bromine?

_____

_____

5. Compare Which property would be easiest to use to distinguish chlorine from the other gases in the table? Explain your reasoning.

_____

_____

6. Identify A white solid melts at 740°C. Could the substance be table salt (sodium chloride)? Explain your reasoning.

_____

_____

7. Draw Conclusions Which of the physical properties listed in the table would be the most helpful in identifying substances? *Hint:* Which physical properties are unique to each substance?

_____

_____

2 Standardized Test Prep Tutor

The lettered choices below refer to Questions 6–9. A lettered choice may be used once, more than once, or not at all.

    (A) compound
    (B) heterogeneous mixture
    (C) element
    (D) homogeneous mixture

Which description correctly identifies each of the following materials?

6. air

7. carbon monoxide

8. zinc

9. mushroom pizza

Think of Questions 6–9 as multiple-choice questions, where the answer choices are listed before the question instead of after. The questions have been rewritten as complete sentences that begin "Which description correctly identifies . . ."

6. Which description correctly identifies air?

Air is a mixture of gases. The different types of gases are spread evenly throughout the mixture.

Look at the lettered choices. Which choice describes this type of mixture?

A homogeneous mixture has a uniform composition. So the correct answer is D.

7. Which description correctly identifies carbon monoxide?

Carbon monoxide contains the elements carbon and oxygen. These elements are chemically combined in carbon monoxide.

A compound is a substance that contains two or more elements that are chemically combined. So the correct answer is A.

8. Which description correctly identifies zinc?

Zinc is a metal that cannot be broken down into simpler substances.

An element is the simplest form of matter that has a unique set of properties. So the correct answer is C.

Now you try it.

9. Which description correctly identifies mushroom pizza?

_____

_____

_____

Use the atomic windows to answer Question 10. The key terms have been highlighted for you.

(A)   (B)   (C)   (D)

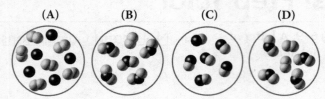

10. The species in window A react. Use the law of conservation of mass to determine which window best represents the reaction products.

❶ Analyze

Each chemical species contains a single type of particle or a specific combination of particles. Window A contains two chemical species. One is represented by white particles that are combined in pairs. The other is represented by single black particles. Count each individual particle, whether it is shown as a single particle or combined with other particles.

There are ____ white particles in window A.

There are ____ black particles in window A.

❷ Solve

According to the law of conservation of mass, the atomic window showing the reaction products must contain the same number of each type of particle as window A. Count the number of white particles and black particles in windows B, C, and D.

❸ Choose an Answer

Which window has the same number of white particles and black particles as window A?

Window B contains the same number of each particle as window A.

Now you try it.

(A)   (B)   (C)   (D)

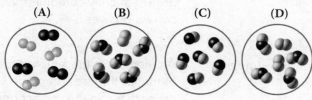

A reaction takes place between the chemical species in window A. Use the law of conservation of mass to determine which window best represents the reaction products.

_____

_____

_____

_____

_____

More Practice Using Scientific Notation   Lesson 3.1

Step-by-Step Practice

1. What is the mass, in kilograms, of a star that is
   1.5×10^2 times the mass of the Sun? The Sun's mass is
   2.0×10^{30} kg. Express the answer in scientific notation.

   ❶ Analyze Identify the relevant concepts.

   Multiply numbers written in scientific notation by
   multiplying the coefficients and then adding the
   exponents.

   ❷ Solve Apply the concepts to this problem.

Set up the problem.	$(2.0 \times 10^{30}) \times (1.5 \times 10^2)$
Multiply the coefficients.	$(2.0 \times 10^{30}) \times (1.5 \times 10^2)$
	$(2.0 \times 1.5) = 3.0$
Then add the exponents.	$(2.0 \times 10^{30}) \times (1.5 \times 10^2) =$
	$(10^{30} \times 10^2) = 10^{30\,+\,2} = 10^{32}$
Combine the results of the two operations.	$(2.0 \times 10^{30}) \times (1.5 \times 10^2) = 3.0 \times 10^{32}$

   The star's mass is 3.0×10^{32} kg.

2. What is the mass of a star that is equal to the Sun's mass
   divided by 1.5×10^{-2}? The Sun's mass is 2.0×10^{30} kg.
   Express the answer in scientific notation.

   ❶ Analyze Identify the relevant concepts.

   Divide numbers written in scientific notation by dividing
   the coefficients and then subtracting the exponents.

   ❷ Solve Apply the concepts to this problem.

Set up the problem.	$(\underline{\hspace{1cm}} \times 10^{30}) \div (\underline{\hspace{1cm}} \times 10^{-2})$
Divide the coefficients.	$(\underline{\hspace{1cm}} \div 1.5) = \underline{\hspace{1cm}}$
Then subtract the exponents.	$(10^{30} \div 10^{-2}) = 10^{30\,-\,(-2)}$
Combine the results of the two operations.	$(2.0 \times 10^{30}) \div (1.5 \times 10^{-2}) = \underline{\hspace{1cm}} \times \underline{\hspace{1cm}}$

   The star's mass is _____.

3. The population of California is 3.7×10^7 people. The population of Colorado is 5.0×10^6 people. What is the difference in size between these two populations? Express the answer in scientific notation.

❶ Analyze Identify the relevant concepts.

To subtract numbers written in scientific notation, rewrite the numbers so the exponents are the same and then subtract the coefficients.

❷ Solve Apply the concepts to this problem.

Write the expression for subtraction. Then rewrite the numbers so the exponents are the same.

$(3.7 \times 10^7) - ($ _____ $)$

$(3.7 \times 10^7) - ($ _____ $\times 10^7)$

Subtract the coefficients.

$3.7 -$ _____ $=$ _____

The difference in population is _____ people.

On Your Own

4. Express the answers to the following problems in scientific notation. *Hint:* Use the subtraction example to solve the addition problem.

a. $(1.8 \times 10^{20}) \times (4.5 \times 10^{16})$ **c.** $(9.2 \times 10^{19}) \div (4.0 \times 10^7)$

    a. _____   **c.** _____

b. $(7.9 \times 10^9) - (3.0 \times 10^8)$ **d.** $(4.2 \times 10^{19}) + (6.0 \times 10^{18})$

    b. _____   **d.** _____

5. The density of a substance is 3.4×10^3 g/mL. Mixing it with another substance increases the density by 1.5×10^1 times. What is the density of the mixture?

6. A compound contains atoms of sulfur and iron. There are 3.6×10^{20} atoms of iron in the compound. Divide the number of iron atoms by 1.8×10^{-5} to find the number of sulfur atoms in the compound.

More Practice Significant Figures in Calculations
Lesson 3.1

Step-by-Step Practice

1. Find the area of a vegetable garden that is 4.83 meters long and 3.4 meters wide. Give the answer to the correct number of significant figures.

❶ **Analyze** Identify the relevant concepts.

After doing the math operation, round the answer to match the measurement with the least number of significant figures.

❷ **Solve** Apply the concepts to this problem.

Multiply the measurements to find the area. Be sure to include the units in your calculation.

$4.83 \text{ m} \times 3.4 \text{ m} = 16.422 \text{ m}^2$

Identify the measurement with the least number of significant figures. That measurement is 3.4 m, which has two significant figures. Round the answer to two significant figures.

$16.422 \text{ m} \longrightarrow 16 \text{ m}^2$

....

2. A contractor uses 16 tiles to cover a bathroom floor that has an area of 2.4283 m². What is the area of each tile? Give the answer to the correct number of significant figures.

❶ **Analyze** Identify the relevant concepts.

After doing the math operation, round the answer to match the measurement with the least number of significant figures.

❷ **Solve** Apply the concepts to this problem.

Divide the area by the number of tiles. Be sure to include the units in your calculation.

$2.4283 \text{ m}^2 \div$ _____ tiles = _____ m²/tile

Identify the measurement with the least number of significant figures. How many significant figures does that measurement have? Round the answer to match that number of significant figures.

_____ significant figures

_____ m²/tile

On Your Own

3. After doing each operation, round the answer to the correct number of significant figures.

a. 1.6 meters × 48.302 meters

c. 267.2298 meters^2 ÷ 8.2 meters

a. _____

c. _____

b. 43.2 cm × 0.0062 cm

d. 1001.3 cm^2 ÷ 6.15 cm

b. _____

d. _____

4. The area (A) of a rectangle is the product of its length and width (l × w). Find the area of the rectangle that is formed by each pair of measurements. Round each answer to the correct number of significant figures.

a. l = 3.4 m; w = 11.6 m

c. l = 1.386 cm; w = 2.4 cm

Area = _____

Area = _____

b. l = 15.3 m; w = 1.862 m

d. l = 83.005 cm; w = 6.280 cm

Area = _____

Area = _____

Interpret Data Comparing Densities

Lesson 3.2

Preview the Tables

The tables show the densities of some common liquids and gases. Recall that density is a ratio that compares the mass of a material to its volume.

Look at the table of densities for common gases. The densities are given at 20°C. What unit is used for the density of a gas?

_____

Look at the table of densities for common liquids. The unit of density for the liquids is grams per cubic centimeter. For all but one liquid, the density is given at 20°C. For which liquid is the density given at 4°C?

_____

For all but one liquid, there is a ≈ symbol in front of the density. This symbol means "about." For instance, the density of vegetable oil, at 20°C, is about 0.91 g/cm³.

Densities of Some Common Gases	
Material	**Density at 20°C (g/L)**
Carbon dioxide	1.83
Oxygen	1.33
Air	1.20
Nitrogen	1.17
Methane	0.665
Helium	0.166
Hydrogen	0.084

Densities of Some Common Liquids	
Material	**Density at 20°C (g/cm³)**
Vegetable oil	≈ 0.91
Water (4°C)	1.000
Dish soap	≈ 1.03
Corn syrup	≈ 1.33
Honey	≈ 1.36

Analyze the Table

Now you are ready to answer some more questions. As you read the questions:

► Highlight key words.
► Circle numbers and units.

Use the first question as an example.

1. Read Tables Which liquid in the table is the most dense? What is the density of this material?

_____

2. Predict If honey and water are placed in the same container, which material will form the top layer?

_____

> **Try it!** Look at the table for liquids. The liquids are listed from top to bottom in order from least dense to most dense.

> **Try it!** Find the density for water and the density for honey. Of the two materials, the one that is less dense will form the top layer.

3. Compare Which gas is twice as dense as methane at 20°C?

_____

_____

> **Try it!** Find the density of methane and multiply it by 2. Then find the gas with a density that matches your answer.

On Your Own

4. Read Tables Which gas has a greater density, air or carbon dioxide?

_____

5. Compare Which gas is about half as dense as helium?

_____

6. Predict Would a balloon filled with carbon dioxide sink or rise in air? Explain.

_____

_____

7. Apply Concepts Why do you think that water is the only material in the liquids table without a ≈ symbol? *Hint:* Think about how you classified materials in Chapter 2?

_____

_____

More Practice Converting Between Metric Units
Lesson 3.3

Step-by-Step Practice

1. Convert 685 nm to μm.

❶ **Analyze** List the knowns and the unknown.

Knowns	Unknown
length = 685 nm	length = ? μm
1 m = 10^9 nm	
1 m = 10^6 μm	

❷ **Calculate** Solve for the unknown.

Set up the conversion factors. In this case, you can convert nm to m and then convert m to μm.

$$\frac{1 \text{ m}}{10^9 \text{ nm}} \qquad \frac{10^6 \text{ μm}}{1 \text{ m}}$$

Multiply the known length by the conversion factors. Cross out units that are in both the numerator and the denominator. Then write the length with the correct units.

$$685 \text{ nm} \times \frac{1 \text{ m}}{10^9 \text{ nm}} \times \frac{10^6 \text{ μm}}{1 \text{ m}} = 0.685 \text{ μm}$$

❸ **Evaluate** Does the result make sense?

A micrometer is longer than a nanometer. So it makes sense that the number of micrometers is less than the number of nanometers. The answer has the correct units and the correct number of significant figures.

. . . .

2. Convert a mass of 380 mg to dg.

❶ **Analyze** List the knowns and the unknown.

Knowns	Unknown
mass = _____	mass = ? dg
1 g = 10^3 mg	
1 g = 10 dg	

❷ **Calculate** Solve for the unknown.

Set up the conversion factors. In this case, you can convert mg to g and then convert g to dg.

$$\frac{1 \text{ g}}{10^3 \text{ mg}} \qquad \frac{10 \text{ dg}}{1 \text{ g}}$$

Multiply the known mass by each conversion factor. Cross out units that are in both the numerator and the denominator. Then write the mass with the correct units.

$$380 \text{ mg} \times \frac{1 \text{ g}}{10^3 \text{ mg}} \times \frac{10 \text{ dg}}{1 \text{ g}} = \underline{\quad} \text{ dg}$$

❸ **Evaluate** Does the result make sense?

_____

_____

_____

On Your Own

3. A measure of electrical current in milliamps is written as 645 mA. Write the measurement of the current in amps. *Hint:* 1 amp = 1000 milliamps.

4. The difference between the first and second place race times at a swim meet is 0.0520 s. Write this time difference in milliseconds (ms).

5. A mechanical pencil is 14 cm long. What is its length in mm?

More Practice Using Density as a Conversion Factor

Lesson 3.3

Step-by-Step Practice

1. A block of iron (Fe) has a volume of 15.8 cm³ and a density of 7.85 g/cm³. What is its mass?

❶ Analyze List the knowns and the unknown.

Knowns	Unknown
volume of iron = 15.8 cm³	mass = ? g
density of iron = 7.85 g/cm³	

❷ Calculate Solve for the unknown.

Use the density and volume of iron to find the mass of the block of iron. Write a conversion factor to convert volume to mass. The known unit (cm³) should be in the denominator.

$$\frac{7.85 \text{ g}}{1 \text{ cm}^3}$$

Multiply the volume of the iron block by the conversion factor.

$$15.8 \text{ cm}^3 \text{ Fe} \times \frac{7.85 \text{ g Fe}}{1 \text{ cm}^3 \text{ Fe}} = 124.03 \text{ g Fe}$$

Round your answer to the correct number of significant figures.

124.03 g Fe ⟶ 124 g Fe

❸ Evaluate Does the result make sense?

A volume of 1 cm³ of iron has a mass of 7.85 g. So it makes sense that a volume almost 16 times greater would have a mass that is almost 16 times greater than 7.85 g. The answer has three significant figures because both knowns have three significant figures.

....

2. A metal statue has a density of 6.18 g/cm³. What is the volume of the statue if its mass is 2250 g?

❶ Analyze List the knowns and the unknown.

Knowns	Unknown
mass of metal = _____	volume = ? cm³
density of metal = _____	

❷ **Calculate** **Solve for the unknown.**

Use the density to find the volume of the statue. $\dfrac{1\ cm^3}{6.18\ g}$
Write a conversion factor to convert mass to volume.
The known unit should be in the denominator.

Multiply the mass of the metal statue   2250 g metal × ——————— = _____ cm³ metal
by the conversion factor.

Round your answer to the correct number of   _____ cm³ metal
significant figures.

❸ **Evaluate** **Does the result make sense?**

_____

_____

_____

_____

On Your Own

3. A solid cylinder of metal has a volume of 21.6 cm³ and mass of 193 g. The cylinder is cut
into two pieces. What is the density of each piece? *Hint:* Cutting the cylinder into two
pieces has no effect on its density.

4. A student wants to compare the volumes of two metal blocks. Block A has a mass of
128.45 g and a density of 8.80 g/cm³. Block B has a mass of 92.2 g and a density of
7.14 g/cm³. Which block has a greater volume? Show your calculations.

3 Standardized Test Prep Tutor

Read the question. The term with the blue highlight tells you how many significant figures need to be in the answer.

2. Which answer represents the measurement 0.00428 g rounded to two significant figures?
   (A) 4.28×10^3 g   (C) 4.3×10^{-3} g
   (B) 4.3×10^3 g   (D) 4.0×10^{-3} g

❶ Analyze

Since all the answers are in scientific notation, you first need to convert the measurement to scientific notation. Then you can round the answer to two significant figures.

❷ Solve

Move the decimal point to the right until you have a number that is greater than 1 but less than 10. The value of the exponent is the number of places the decimal point has been moved. The exponent will be negative because you moved the decimal point to the right.

0.00428 g $=$ _____ $\times 10^{-3}$ g

Round the measurement to two significant digits. The last digit is greater than 5, so increase the value of the last significant digit by 1.

_____ $\times 10^{-3}$ g $\cong$ _____ $\times 10^{-3}$ g

❸ Choose an Answer

Look at the answer choices. Find the choice that matches your calculation. The correct answer is C.

Now you try it.

Which answer represents the measurement 0.02023 m rounded to three significant figures?
   (A) 2.023×10^2 m   (C) 2.23×10^{-2} m
   (B) 2.02×10^2 m   (D) 2.02×10^{-2} m

Read the question. The highlighted term tells you what you need to find. Circle any numbers and units.

7. A graduated cylinder contains 44.2 mL of water. A 48.6-g piece of metal is carefully dropped into the cylinder. When the metal is completely covered with water, the water rises to the 51.3 mL mark. What is the density of the metal?

❶ Analyze

Use a knowns and unknown table to organize the volume and mass data.

Knowns	Unknown
V_1 = 44.2 mL	density = ? g/cm^3
V_2 = 51.3 mL	
mass = 48.6 g	

Write the equation for density.

$$Density = \frac{mass}{volume}$$

You need to know both the mass and volume of the metal to find its density. You know the mass of the metal, but how can you find its volume? You can find the volume of the metal by subtracting the volume of the water from the volume of the water plus the metal.

❷ Solve

Find the volume of the metal. Convert the units from mL to cubic centimeters. Remember that 1 mL = 1 cm^3.

51.3 mL − 44.2 mL = _____ mL

_____ m̶L̶ $\times \dfrac{1\ cm^3}{1\ m̶L̶}$ = _____ cm^3

Substitute the known values into the density equation.

$$Density = \frac{48.6\ g}{7.1\ cm^3} = _____$$

❸ Choose an Answer

Write your answer. Make sure you use the correct number of significant figures in your answer.

Density = _____

Now you try it.

A graduated cylinder contains 59.1 mL of water. A 74.9-g piece of metal is carefully dropped into the cylinder. When the metal is completely covered with water, the water rises to the 67.5 mL mark. What is the density of the metal?

$$Density = _____ = _____$$

More Practice Determining the Composition of an Atom   Lesson 4.3

Step-by-Step Practice

1. How many protons, electrons, and neutrons are in an atom of $^{64}_{29}Cu$?

❶ Analyze List the knowns and the unknowns.

In a chemical symbol, the lower number represents the atomic number of the atom. The upper number represents the mass number of the atom.

Knowns	Unknowns
Copper (Cu)	number of protons = ?
atomic number = 29	number of electrons = ?
mass number = 64	number of neutrons = ?

❷ Calculate Solve for the unknowns.

Use the atomic number to find the number of protons.

atomic number = number of protons
= 29

Use the number of protons to find the number of electrons. Because an atom is neutral, the number of electrons must equal the number of protons.

number of protons = number of electrons
= 29

Subtract the atomic number from the mass number to find the number of neutrons.

mass number − atomic number =
number of neutrons = 64 − 29 = 35

....

2. How many protons, electrons, and neutrons are in an atom of $^{65}_{30}Zn$?

❶ Analyze List the knowns and the unknowns.

Knowns	Unknowns
Zinc (Zn)	number of protons = ?
atomic number = _____	number of electrons = ?
mass number = _____	number of neutrons = ?

❷ Calculate **Solve for the unknowns.**

Use the atomic number to find the number of protons.
Then use the number of protons to find the
number of electrons.

atomic number = number of protons =   number of protons = _____
number of electrons   number of electrons = _____

Subtract the atomic number from the mass number   number of neutrons =
to find the number of neutrons.   _____ − _____ = _____

number of neutrons = mass number − atomic number

On Your Own

3. How many protons, electrons, and neutrons are in each atom?
   a. $^{52}_{24}$Cr   b. $^{24}_{12}$Mg

4. How many neutrons does an atom have if it has 31 protons and a mass number of 70?
   What element is it?

5. Write the chemical symbol for each atom. *Hint:* Find the symbol for the element.
   Then write the mass number above the atomic number to the left of that symbol.
   a. number of protons = 55;
      mass number = 133
   b. atomic number = 22;
      mass number = 48

Interpret Data Percent Abundance of Stable Isotopes Lesson 4.3

Preview the Table

Read the title of the table and the column heads. The first column lists six elements. The second column shows symbols for each element. What do these symbols represent?

_____

_____

_____

The third column shows the natural percent abundance of each stable isotope. Natural percent abundance is a measure of the relative amount of one isotope compared to another in nature. Which isotope of oxygen is most abundant in nature?

_____

Natural Percent Abundance of Stable Isotopes of Some Elements				
Name	Symbol	Natural percent abundance	Mass (amu)	Atomic mass (amu)
Hydrogen	^1_1H	99.985	1.0078	1.0079
	^2_1H	0.015	2.0141	
	^3_1H	negligible	3.0160	
Helium	^3_2He	0.0001	3.0160	4.0026
	^3_2He	99.9999	4.0026	
Carbon	$^{12}_6C$	98.89	12.000	12.011
	$^{13}_6C$	1.11	13.003	
Nitrogen	$^{14}_7N$	99.63	14.003	14.007
	$^{15}_7N$	0.37	15.000	
Oxygen	$^{16}_8O$	99.759	15.995	15.999
	$^{17}_8O$	0.037	16.995	
	$^{18}_8O$	0.204	17.999	
Chlorine	$^{35}_{17}Cl$	75.77	34.969	35.453
	$^{37}_{17}Cl$	24.23	36.966	

Each isotope of an element has a different number of neutrons. The fourth column lists the mass of each isotope. How does a change in the number of neutrons affect the mass of each isotope?

_____

_____

Analyze the Table

Now you are ready to answer some more questions. As you read the questions:

► Highlight key words.

► Circle numbers and units.

Use the first question as an example.

1. Read Tables How many isotopes of hydrogen occur naturally?

_____

> **Try it!** Find the row with data for hydrogen. Count the number of isotopes in the Symbol column for that row.

2. Read Tables Which isotope of hydrogen is the most abundant? Explain how you determined your answer.

> Try it! Look for the largest number under Natural percent abundance in the Hydrogen row.

_____

_____

3. Identify What is the mass of the oxygen isotope $^{17}_{8}O$?

> Try it! Find the isotope $^{17}_{8}O$. Move your finger across to the fourth column to find its mass in amu.

_____

_____

On Your Own

4. Read Tables Which isotope of chlorine is most abundant?

_____

5. Draw Conclusions Why is the atomic mass of the element carbon very similar to the mass of the carbon isotope $^{12}_{6}C$?

_____

_____

6. Explain If you didn't know the natural percent abundance of each helium isotope, how could you use the atomic mass of helium to determine which isotope was most abundant?

_____

_____

_____

4 Standardized Test Prep Tutor

Read the question. You are being asked to use the numbers of particles in an atom to find the correct shorthand notation for the atom.

Notes and Calculations

4. Which atom is composed of 16 protons, 16 electrons, and 16 neutrons?

(A) $^{48}_{16}S$ (C) $^{32}_{16}S$

(B) $^{16}_{32}Ge$ (D) $^{16}_{32}S$

❶ Analyze

The shorthand notation for an atom of an element includes the chemical symbol for the element with two numbers written to its left. The bottom number is the atomic number. The top number is the mass number. Find the atomic number and mass number to choose the correct shorthand notation for the atom described in the question.

❷ Solve

The atomic number of an element is the number of protons in an atom of the element. What is the atomic number of this element?

The mass number of an element is the sum of the protons and neutrons in an atom of the element. What is the mass number of this element?

Atomic number = _____

Mass number

= protons + neutrons

= _____ + _____

= _____

❸ Choose an Answer

Look at the answer choices. Which choice shows the correct atomic number and mass number in the correct positions? The correct answer is C.

Now you try it.

4. Which atom is composed of 23 protons, 23 electrons, and 28 neutrons?

(A) $^{51}_{23}V$ (C) $^{23}_{51}V$

(B) $^{46}_{28}Ni$ (D) $^{28}_{46}V$

Use the picture below to answer Question 5.

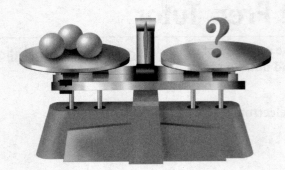

5. How many nitrogen-14 atoms (^{14}N) would you need to place on the right pan to balance the three calcium-42 atoms (^{42}Ca) on the left pan of the "atomic balance" above? Describe the method you used to determine your answer, including any calculations.

❶ Analyze

Find the mass of three ^{42}Ca atoms. Then find the number of ^{14}N atoms that would have the same mass.

❷ Solve

Step 1: Find the mass of one ^{42}Ca atom.

One atom of ^{42}Ca has a total of 42 protons and neutrons. The mass of a single proton or neutron is about 1 amu.

The mass of one ^{42}Ca atom is about 42 amu.

Step 2: Find the mass of three ^{42}Ca atoms.

42 amu × 3 = 126 amu

Step 3: Find the mass of one ^{14}N atom.

The mass of one ^{14}N atom is about 14 amu.

Step 4: Find the number of ^{14}N atoms that have a mass of 126 amu.

126 amu ÷ 14 amu = 9

❸ Choose an Answer

You have already described your method. Now write the answer to the question as a sentence.

You would need nine ^{14}N atoms to balance the three ^{42}Ca atoms.

Now you try it.

An "atomic balance" has three mercury-196 atoms (^{196}Hg) on its left pan. How many titanium-49 atoms (^{49}Ti) would you need to place on the right pan to balance the ^{196}Hg atoms? Describe the method you used to determine your answer.

Method: _____

_____

_____

Answer: _____

_____

More Practice Writing Electron Configurations

Lesson 5.2

Step-by-Step Practice

1. The atomic number for silicon is 14. Write the orbital diagram and electron configuration for a silicon atom.

❶ Analyze Identify the relevant concepts.

Silicon has 14 electrons. These electrons fill atomic orbitals according to the principles and rules described in Lesson 5.2 of your textbook.

❷ Solve Apply the concepts to this problem.

Start with a diagram that shows the orbitals in order of lowest energy to highest energy.

$1s$	$2s$	$2p$	$3s$	$3p$	$4s$
☐	☐	☐ ☐ ☐	☐	☐ ☐ ☐	☐

Place two arrows in each orbital for energy sublevels that can be completely filled. These arrows represent electrons and the direction of their spin. Two electrons in the same orbital must have opposite spins.

$1s$	$2s$	$2p$	$3s$	$3p$	$4s$
↑↓	↑↓	↑↓ ↑↓ ↑↓	↑↓	☐ ☐ ☐	☐

Place arrows in the first two $3p$ orbitals to represent the remaining two electrons. Both arrows should point in the same direction, to show that the electrons have the same spin.

$1s$	$2s$	$2p$	$3s$	$3p$	$4s$
↑↓	↑↓	↑↓ ↑↓ ↑↓	↑↓	↑ ↑ ☐	☐

Write the symbol of each sublevel with a superscript showing the number of electrons.

The electron configuration of silicon is $1s^2 2s^2 2p^6 3s^2 3p^2$.

....

2. The atomic number for chlorine is 17. Write the orbital diagram and electron configuration for a chlorine atom.

❶ Analyze Identify the relevant concepts.

Chlorine has 17 electrons. These electrons fill atomic orbitals according to the principles and rules described in Lesson 5.2 of your textbook.

❷ Solve Apply the concepts to this problem.

Place two arrows in each orbital for energy sublevels that can be completely filled.

$1s$	$2s$	$2p$	$3s$	$3p$	$4s$
☐	☐	☐ ☐ ☐	☐	☐ ☐ ☐	☐

Place arrows to represent any remaining electrons in the next energy sublevel. Place one arrow in each orbital in the sublevel before adding a second arrow to any orbital in that sublevel.

1s	2s	2p	3s	3p	4s
☐	☐	☐☐☐	☐	☐☐☐	☐

Write the symbol of each sublevel with a superscript showing the number of electrons.

The electron configuration of chlorine is _____.

On Your Own

3. The atomic number for neon is 10. Write the orbital diagram and the electron configuration for a neon atom.

4. The atomic number for potassium is 19. Write the orbital diagram and the electron configuration for a potassium atom.

5. The atomic number for zinc is 30. Write the orbital diagram for a zinc atom.
   Hint: Remember that the 4s orbital has lower energy than the 3d orbitals.

5 Standardized Test Prep Tutor

Read the question. Highlight the word silicon and circle the number 14.

3. Select the correct electron configuration for silicon (atomic number 14).
   (A) $1s^2 2s^2 2p^2 3s^2 3p^2 3d^2 4s^2$ **(C)** $1s^2 2s^6 2p^6$
   (B) $1s^2 2s^2 2p^4 3s^2 3p^4$ **(D)** $1s^2 2s^2 2p^6 3s^2 3p^2$

❶ Analyze

Silicon has 14 electrons. The number of electrons in each answer choice is 14. So the correct answer will depend on how the electrons are distributed.

❷ Solve

You can use a process of elimination to find the correct answer. The maximum number of electrons in an *s* orbital is two. Eliminate any answer in which an *s* orbital has more than two electrons.

Answer C is not correct.

In a filled energy level, a *p* sublevel must have 6 electrons. Eliminate any answers in which a *p* sublevel that is not in the highest occupied energy level has fewer than 6 electrons.

Answers A and B are not correct.

❸ Choose an Answer

Look at answer choice D. Each *s* orbital had two electrons. The *p* orbitals in the second energy level have 6 electrons.

The correct answer is D.

Now you try it.

Select the correct electron configuration for potassium (atomic number 19). *Hint:* Check for any missing orbitals.
(A) $1s^2 2s^2 2p^6 3s^2 3d^6 4s^1$ **(C)** $1s^2 2s^2 2p^6 3s^2 3p^6 4s^1$
(B) $1s^2 2s^4 2p^6 3p^6 4s^1$ **(D)** $1s^2 2s^4 2p^6 3s^2 3p^3 4s^1$

Use the drawings to answer Questions 11–14. Each drawing represents an electromagnetic wave. You will be shown how to answer Questions 11 and 12. You will do Questions 13 and 14 on your own.

Waves

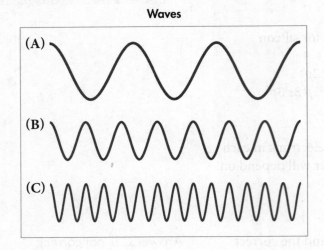

(A)

(B)

(C)

11. Which wave has the longest wavelength?
12. Which wave has the highest energy?
13. Which wave has the lowest frequency?
14. Which wave has the highest amplitude?

Focus on one question at a time. In Questions 11 and 12, the property you will use to identify the correct wave has been highlighted.

11. Which wave has the longest wavelength?

Wavelength is the distance between two crests that are next to each other. Crests are the highest points on a wave.

Look at the drawings of the waves. On each wave, draw a line between two crests. Identify the wave with the longest line. This is the wave with the longest wavelength.

The correct answer is A.

12. Which wave has the highest energy?

Look at the drawings of the waves. Find the wave that has the shortest wavelength and the highest frequency.

The correct answer is C.

Now you try it.

13. Which wave has the lowest frequency?

The correct answer is _____.

14. Which wave has the highest amplitude? *Hint:* Amplitude is the height of the wave.

The correct answer is _____.

Interpret Graphs Atomic Radius vs. Atomic Number   Lesson 6.3

Preview the Graph

Read the title of the graph. This graph shows the relationship between the atomic radius and the atomic numbers of elements 1 through 55. Atomic number is on the *x*-axis. Atomic radius in picometers (pm) is on the *y*-axis. The atomic radius allows you to compare the size of different atoms.

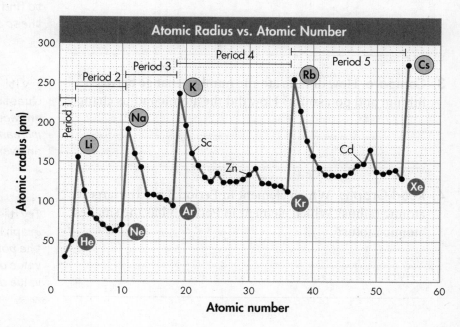

Each point on the graph represents the atomic radius of one element. The gray circles mark the atomic radii of alkali metals.

What do the blue circles mark?

_____

_____

Find the bracket with the label Period 2. This bracket marks the region of the graph with data for elements in Period 2. The bracket with the label Period 3 marks the region of the graph with data for elements in Period 3. How many periods are represented on the graph?

_____

_____

Analyze the Graph

Now you are ready to answer some more questions. As you read the questions:

► Highlight key words.
► Circle numbers and units.

Use the first question as an example.

1. Read Graphs Find the element lithium, Li, on the graph. What is its atomic number? What is its atomic radius?

_____

_____

> **Try it!** Find the point representing Li on the graph. Follow the lines from this point to the x-axis and to the y-axis.

Name _____ Class _____ Date _____

2. Read Graphs Which element has an atomic number of 19 and an atomic radius of 238 pm?

_____

_____

> **Try it!** Find 238 on the y-axis and 19 on the x-axis. Use your fingers to find the point where lines from these data points meet.

3. Compare How did the atomic number change between lithium and potassium? How did the atomic radius change?

_____

_____

> **Try it!** Use your answers to Question 1 and Question 2 to answer Question 3. Use the word *increased* or *decreased* in your answer.

4. Read Graphs Which element in Period 3 has the largest atomic radius? Which element in Period 3 has the smallest atomic radius?

_____

_____

> **Try it!** Look for the section of the graph labeled Period 3. Look for the points that have the greatest value on the y-axis and the least value on the y-axis.

On Your Own

5. Read Graphs Which element in Period 4 has the largest atomic radius? Which element in Period 4 has the smallest atomic radius?

_____

_____

6. Drawing Conclusions From left to right across a period, describe what happens to the atomic size of the elements.

_____

_____

7. Make Generalizations What is the trend for atomic size within a group? *Hint:* Look at the points for the alkali metals. Then look at the points for the noble gases.

_____

_____

_____

8. Predicting The graph stops with cesium (Cs), which has an atomic number of 55. Barium has an atomic number of 56. Would the atomic radius of barium be larger or smaller than the atomic radius of cesium? Explain your reasoning.

_____

_____

_____

Interpret Graphs

First Ionization Energy vs. Atomic Number

Lesson 6.3

Preview the Graph

Read the title of the graph. This graph relates an element's position on the periodic table to its first ionization energy. This energy is the energy needed to remove the first electron from an atom. First ionization energy in kJ/mol is the variable on the y-axis. A mole (mol) is the amount of matter equal to the atomic mass of an element in grams.

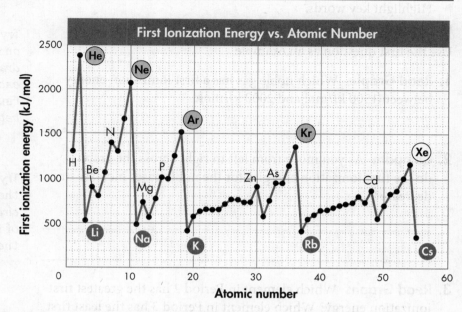

First Ionization Energy vs. Atomic Number

Atomic number is the variable on the x-axis. What happens to the atomic number as you move from left to right across the graph?

_____

_____

Find the points that represent the group of noble gases. These points are marked by gray circles with symbols for noble gases. Find the points that represent the group of alkali metals. How are these points marked?

_____

_____

How does the graph change between He and Li? How does the graph change between Li and Ne?

_____

_____

_____

Analyze the Graph

Now you are ready to answer some more questions. As you read the questions:

▶ Highlight key words.
▶ Circle numbers and units.

Use the first question as an example.

1. Read Graphs Which noble gas has a first ionization energy between 1500 kJ/mol and 2000 kJ/mol?

_____

> **Try it!** Find 1500 and 2000 on the y-axis. Use a pencil to draw a horizontal line from each point across the graph. Find the noble gas located *between* the lines.

2. Compare As you move from left to right across the graph, do the first ionization energies for the noble gases increase or decrease?

_____

_____

> **Try it!** The noble gases are the points marked by gray circles. Compare the position of these points relative to the y-axis.

3. Read Graphs Which element in Period 2 has the greatest first ionization energy? Which element in Period 3 has the least first ionization energy?

_____

_____

> **Try it!** Look for the points in Period 2 and Period 3 that have the lowest position relative to the y-axis.

On Your Own

4. Compare As you move from left to right across the graph, do the first ionization energies for the alkali metals increase or decrease?

_____

5. Make Generalizations What happens to the first ionization energy within a group as the atomic number increases? Begin your sentence with "As the atomic number increases…."

_____

_____

6. Make Generalizations What tends to happen to the first ionization energy as the atomic number increases across a period?

_____

_____

Interpret Data Ionization Energies

Lesson 6.3

Preview the Table

The table compares ionization energies for elements 1 through 14. Look at the title of the graph. What unit is used for ionization energy?

_____

_____

Symbols for the elements are listed on the left. The column titled First lists the first ionization energy for each element. Recall that the first ionization energy is the energy needed to remove the first electron from an atom. The Second column lists the energy needed to remove a second electron from an atom. What does the Third column list?

Ionization Energies of First 14 Elements (kJ/mol)			
Symbol	First	Second	Third
H	1312		
He (noble gas)	2372	5247	
Li	520	7297	11,810
Be	899	1757	14,840
B	801	2430	3659
C	1086	2352	4619
N	1402	2857	4577
O	1314	3391	5301
F	1681	3375	6045
Ne (noble gas)	2080	3963	6276
Na	496	4565	6912
Mg	738	1450	7732
Al	578	1816	2744
Si	786	1577	3229

Find the two blue lines that zigzag across the table. The first blue line passes just below the first ionization energy for helium (He), the second ionization energy for lithium (Li), and the third ionization energy for beryllium (Be). Describe the position of the second blue line.

_____

_____

Analyze the Table

Now you are ready to answer some more questions. As you read the questions:

► Highlight key words.
► Circle numbers and units.

Use the first question as an example.

1. **Read Tables** What is the symbol of the element that has a first ionization energy of 2372 kJ/mol and a second ionization energy of 5247 kJ/mol?

_____

Try it! Find the row in the table with the value 2372 in the First column and the value 5247 in the Second column.

2. Compare For the elements in the table, how does the first ionization energy compare to the second ionization energy? How does the second ionization energy compare to the third ionization energy?

_____

_____

_____

_____

> **Try it!** Beginning with lithium (Li), look at the values in the First column, the Second column, and the Third column. Use "is greater than" or "is less than" in your answer.

3. Compare How does the first ionization energy change from one element to the next in Group 1A and Group 2A?

_____

_____

> **Try it!** Find the first ionization energies for lithium (Li) and sodium (Na). Then find the first ionization energies for beryllium (Be) and magnesium (Mg).

On Your Own

4. Read Tables What are the first ionization energies for helium and lithium? What are the first ionization energies for neon and sodium?

_____

_____

5. Draw Conclusions What happens to the first ionization energy between the last element in one period and the first element in the next period?

_____

6. Predict Is lithium or beryllium more likely to form an ion with a 2+ charge? Explain your answer. *Hint:* Look at the second ionization energies.

_____

_____

_____

7. Apply Concepts Use your understanding of ionization energy to explain why hydrogen does not have a second ionization energy and why helium does not have a third ionization energy.

_____

_____

_____

Standardized Test Prep Tutor

Use the spheres to answer Questions 4 and 5. You will be
shown how to solve Question 4. Then you will solve Question 5
on your own.

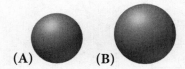

(A)   (B)

4. If the spheres represent a potassium atom and a potassium
ion, which best represents the ion?

❶ Analyze

To choose the correct sphere, you need to recall what kind
of ion potassium forms and then decide whether that ion
will be larger or smaller than a potassium atom.

❷ Solve

Potassium is an alkali metal. Metals tend to lose electrons
and form cations. A cation is smaller than the atom from
which it forms.

❸ Choose an Answer

Look at the spheres. Sphere A is smaller than sphere B. So
Sphere A represents the potassium ion.

Now you try it.

5. If the spheres represent an atom and an anion of the same
element, which sphere represents the atom and which
represents the anion?

_____

_____

_____

The cation has more protons
than electrons. So the attraction
between the remaining electrons
and the nucleus increases.

Use the data table to answer Questions 6–8. You will be shown
how to solve Questions 6 and 7. Then you will solve Question 8
on your own.

Alkali metal	Atomic radius (pm)	First ionization energy (kJ/mol)	Electronegativity value
Li	152	520	1.0
Na	186	495.8	0.9
K	227	418.8	0.8
Rb	244	250	0.8
Cs	262	210	0.7

**Focus on one question at a time. In each question you need to
determine the type of relationship between two variables.**

6. If you plot atomic radius versus first ionization energy,
   would the graph reveal a direct or inverse relationship?

   In a *direct* relationship, if one variable increases, the other
   variable decreases. In an *inverse* relationship, an increase in
   one variable leads to a decrease in the other variable.

   The word *inverse* means
   "opposite."

   You can use the data in the table. You do not have to plot the
   data on a graph. Look at the Atomic radius column. As you
   move down the column from lithium to cesium, the values
   for the atomic radius increase.

   Now look at the values for first ionization energy. As you
   move down the column, the values decrease. The data shows
   that an increase in atomic radius leads to a decrease in first
   ionization energy.

   Atomic radius and first ionization
   energy have an inverse
   relationship.

7. If you plot atomic radius versus electronegativity, would the
   graph reveal a direct or inverse relationship?

   The values for atomic radius increase from lithium to
   cesium. Do the values for electronegativity increase or
   decrease from lithium to cesium?

   The values for electronegativity

   _____.

   Is the relationship between atomic radius and
   electronegativity a direct or an inverse relationship?

   The relationship is _____.

   Now you try it.

8. If you were to plot first ionization energy versus
   electronegativity, would the graph reveal a direct or inverse
   relationship?

   _____

   _____

More Practice Predicting Formulas of Ionic Compounds   Lesson 7.2

Step-by-Step Practice

1. Use electron dot structures to predict the formula of the ionic compound formed from magnesium and bromine.

   ① Analyze Identify the relevant concepts.

   Atoms of metals lose valence electrons when forming an ionic compound. Atoms of nonmetals gain electrons. The final product is electrically neutral.

   ② Solve Apply the concepts to this problem.

   Draw the electron dot structures for magnesium and bromine.

   Mg and $\cdot Br\!:$

   Identify the number of electrons each atom must gain or lose to reach a noble gas electron configuration.

   A magnesium atom must lose two electrons.
   A bromine atom must gain one electron.

   Find the whole number ratio of magnesium to bromine atoms that allows the electrons lost to equal the electrons gained.

   $$Mg + \begin{matrix} \cdot Br\!: \\ \cdot Br\!: \end{matrix} \longrightarrow Mg^{2+} \begin{matrix} :Br\!:^- \\ :Br\!:^- \end{matrix}$$

   Write the ratio as a chemical formula.

   The formula of the ionic compound formed is $MgBr_2$.

....

2. Use electron dot structures to predict the formula of the ionic compound formed from potassium and phosphorus.

   ① Analyze Identify the relevant concepts.

   Atoms of metals lose valence electrons when forming an ionic compound. Atoms of nonmetals gain electrons. The final product is electrically neutral.

   ② Solve Apply the concepts to this problem.

   Draw the electron dot structures for the starting elements.

   Identify the number of electrons each atom must gain or lose to reach a noble gas electron configuration.

   A potassium atom must lose _____ electron(s).

   A phosphorus atom must gain _____ electron(s).

Find the whole number ratio of potassium to phosphorus atoms that allows the electrons lost to equal the electrons gained.

Write the ratio as a chemical formula.

The formula of the ionic compound formed is _____.

On Your Own

3. An ionic compound formed by combining lithium and bromine atoms is used to reduce moisture in air conditioning systems. The diagram below shows the electron dot structure for each atom in the compound. Fill in the rest of the diagram to represent the whole number ratio of lithium to bromine atoms in this compound.

Li• + •B̈r: ⟶

Based on this diagram, what is the formula for the compound?

_____

4. What is the ratio of sodium and sulfur atoms that can combine to form an ionic compound? Use electron dot structures to represent atoms or ions.

5. Aluminum and chlorine atoms combine to form the ionic compound aluminum chloride—a common ingredient in antiperspirant. Determine the ratio of each type of atom that can combine to form the compound. Use electron dot structures to represent atoms or ions. Then write the chemical formula for the compound.

_____

7 Standardized Test Prep Tutor

Read the question. The highlighted words tell you the elements that are involved in the reaction.

2. Which statements are correct when barium and oxygen react to form an ionic compound?
   I. Each barium atom loses 2 electrons and forms a cation.
   II. Oxygen atoms form oxide anions (O^{2-}).
   III. The ions are present in a one-to-one ratio in the compound.

   (A) I and II only   **(C)** I and III only
   (B) II and III only   **(D)** I, II, and III

❶ Analyze

Decide which of the statements labeled I, II, and III are correct. More than one statement may be correct.

❷ Solve

Barium belongs to Group 2A. Elements in this group form ions by losing 2 electrons. A cation is an ion with a positive charge, which forms when an atom loses electrons. Statement I is correct.

Oxygen is in Group 6A. Group 6A elements form anions by gaining two electrons to have a 2− charge. Statement II is correct.

A barium ion has a charge of 2+. An oxide ion has a charge of 2−. One barium ion would combine with one oxygen ion to form a compound with a charge of 0. Statement III is correct.

❸ Choose an Answer

Find the answer choice that includes all three statements. The correct answer is D.

Now you try it.

Which statements are correct when potassium and sulfur react to form an ionic compound?
   I. Each potassium atom loses 1 electron and forms a cation.
   II. Sulfur atoms form sulfide anions (S^{2-}).
   III. The ions are present in a one-to-one ratio in the compound.

   (A) I and II only   **(C)** I and III only
   (B) II and III only   **(D)** I, II, and III

<u>Notes and Calculations</u>

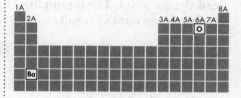

Read the question. Highlight the type of ion.

8. Which electron configuration represents a nitride ion?
   (A) $1s^22s^23s^24s^2$ **(C)** $1s^22s^22p^3$
   (B) $1s^22s^22p^6$ **(D)** $1s^2$

   You do not have to write the electron configuration. You just need to add the exponents in the configurations to find the number of electrons in each answer.

   The electron configuration for nitrogen is $1s^22s^22p^3$. Nitrogen forms a nitride ion by gaining 3 electrons. A nitride ion has 10 electrons.

   Look at the answers. In which choice do the exponents sum to 10? The correct answer is B.

   Now you try it.

   Which electron configuration represents a fluoride ion?
   (A) $1s^22s^22p^63s^2$ **(C)** $1s^22s^22p^4$
   (B) $1s^22s^22p^6$ **(D)** $1s^22s^22p^5$

Read the question. The highlighted term provides an action. You need to figure out the result.

9. When a bromine atom gains an electron
   (A) a bromide ion is formed.
   (B) the ion formed has a 1− charge.
   (C) the ion formed is an anion.
   (D) all the above are correct.

   Answer D includes the other answers. So, you cannot just pick the first correct answer. You must consider all the answers.

   Atoms that gain electrons become anions. The name of an anion ends in –ide. Answer A is correct.

   Elements belonging to Group 7A form ions by gaining one electron, which gives a 1− charge. Answer B is correct.

   An anion is formed when atoms gain electrons, so answer C is correct.

   Answers A, B, and C are correct. So the correct answer is D.

   Now you try it.

   When a selenium atom gains two electrons
   (A) a selenide ion is formed.
   (B) the ion formed has a 2+ charge.
   (C) the ion formed is a cation.
   (D) all the above are correct.

More Practice Drawing an Electron Dot Structure   Lesson 8.2

Step-by-Step Practice

1. Draw the electron dot structure for HBr.

❶ Analyze Identify the relevant concepts.

Atoms that do not have a noble gas electron configuration bond with other atoms to provide the missing electrons. Covalent bonds form when atoms share electrons so each can have the electrons it needs. In a single covalent bond, each atom contributes one electron to the bond. The atoms share the pair of electrons.

❷ Solve Apply the concepts to this problem.

Draw the electron dot structure for each atom. The group number on the periodic table gives the number of electrons to draw.

Hydrogen is in Group 1A. It has 1 electron.

Bromine is in Group 7A. It has 7 electrons.

Determine the number of electrons needed for each atom to have a noble gas configuration. Find the nearest noble gas on the periodic table in Group 8A.

Helium has 2 valence electrons.

Krypton has 8 valence electrons.

Draw the two structures next to each other and put the electrons that are shared on top of each other, or replace the shared electrons with a line.

$$H \cdot \qquad \cdot \overset{\cdot\cdot}{\underset{\cdot\cdot}{Br}} \colon$$

Hydrogen   Bromine
atom   atom

H needs 1 electron to have the electron configuration of He.

Br needs 1 electron to have the electron configuration of Kr.

$$H \colon \overset{\cdot\cdot}{\underset{\cdot\cdot}{Br}} \colon \quad or \quad H - \overset{\cdot\cdot}{\underset{\cdot\cdot}{Br}} \colon$$

Hydrogen bromide molecule

2. Draw the electron-dot structure of NF_3.

❶ Analyze Identify the relevant concepts.

Four atoms will share electrons to form covalent bonds between them. Each atom needs to obtain a noble gas electron configuration.

❷ **Solve** **Apply the concepts to this problem.**

List the number of electrons each atom has. Draw the
electron dot structures for one nitrogen atom and three
fluorine atoms.

Nitrogen is in Group 5A. It has _____ electrons.

Fluorine is in Group 7A. It has _____ electrons.

Determine how many electrons are needed for the
atoms to have a noble gas configuration.

_____ is the nearest noble gas to both elements and
it has _____ electrons.

:N·   ·F: ·F: ·F:

Nitrogen   3 Fluorine atoms
atom

Nitrogen needs _____ electrons.
Each fluorine needs _____ electron.

Arrange the electron structures so each atom has the
number of electrons it needs by sharing electrons.

On Your Own

3. Hydrogen selenide, H_2Se, is used in the semiconductor manufacturing process. Draw the
electron dot structure of hydrogen selenide.

4. Silicon tetrachloride, $SiCl_4$, is used to manufacture extremely pure silicon chips for the
computer industry. Draw the electron dot structure for $SiCl_4$.

5. Draw the electron structure of the ammonium ion (NH_4^+). *Hint:* Ammonium ions
are formed when an ammonia molecule (NH_3) bonds with a hydrogen ion (H^+).
The resulting ion has a positive charge.

8 Standardized Test Prep Tutor

Read the question. The highlighted word tells you what you need to find.

2. How many valence electrons are in a molecule of phosphoric acid (H_3PO_4)?
(A) 7   (C) 24
(B) 16   (D) 32

❶ Analyze

For an element in Group A on the periodic table, the group number tells you the number of valence electrons.

Hydrogen belongs to Group 1A.

Phosphorus belongs to Group 5A.

Oxygen belongs to Group 6A.

Hydrogen has 1 valence electron.

Phosphorus has 5 valence electrons.

Oxygen has 6 valence electrons.

❷ Solve

Multiply the number of atoms of each element by the number of valence electrons for that element.

H: 3×1 valence electron = 3 valence electrons

P: 1×5 valence electrons = 5 valence electrons

O: 4×6 valence electrons = 24 valence electrons

Add the number of valence electrons for the molecule.

$(3 + 5 + 24)$ valence electrons = 32 valence electrons

❸ Choose an Answer

Look at the answer choices. Find the choice that matches your calculations. The correct answer is D.

Now you try it.

How many valence electrons are in a molecule of carbonic acid (H_2CO_3)?
(A) 6   (C) 24
(B) 12   (D) 28

In Questions 12–14, a statement is followed by an explanation. Decide if each statement is true, and then decide if the explanation given is correct. The word "because" separates the statement from the explanation.

You will be shown how to solve Questions 12 and 13. Then you will solve Question 14 on your own.

12. A carbon monoxide molecule has a triple covalent bond because carbon and oxygen atoms have an unequal number of valence electrons.

In a carbon monoxide molecule (CO), an atom of carbon and an atom of oxygen share three pairs of electrons.

> The statement that a carbon monoxide molecule has a triple covalent bond is true.

Now consider the explanation. Nitrogen atoms have the same number of valence electrons. Yet nitrogen atoms form a triple bond in a nitrogen molecule.

> The explanation is not correct.

13. Xenon has a lower boiling point than neon because dispersion forces between xenon atoms are stronger than those between neon atoms.

Sometimes you need to analyze the explanation before you can decide if the statement is true.

By looking at the periodic table, you can tell that xenon atoms have more electrons than neon atoms. So dispersion forces between xenon atoms are stronger.

> The explanation is correct.

Because there is a greater attraction between xenon atoms than between neon atoms, the boiling point of xenon is higher.

> The statement that xenon has a lower boiling point is false.

Now you try it.

14. The nitrate ion has three resonance structures because the nitrate ion has three single bonds.

_____

_____

_____

_____

_____

More Practice Writing Formulas for Ionic Compounds   Lesson 9.2

Step-by-Step Practice

1. Write the formula for calcium iodide, a binary ionic compound.

   ❶ Analyze Identify the relevant concepts.

   Binary ionic compounds are made of a cation and an anion, each made of just one type of atom. The cation is written first in the formula. The ions must be combined in the lowest whole-number ratio possible, and the charges must balance.

   ❷ Solve Apply the concepts to this situation.

   Write the symbol and charge for each ion, with the cation first.

   Ca^{2+} and I^-

   Write the formula using the crisscross method by switching the charges of each ion. The subscript 1 on Ca isn't needed in the formula.

   To check that the formula is correct, multiply the charge of each ion by the number of those ions and add the two parts.

   Evaluate the total charge of CaI_2: 1 Ca ion with a charge of $+2$ and 2 I ions with a charge of -1.

   $1(+2) + 2(-1) = 0$

2. Write the formula for lead(IV) oxide, a binary ionic compound.

   ❶ Analyze Identify the relevant concepts.

   Lead ions can have different charges. The Roman numeral (IV) indicates the charge of the lead ion in this case. The cation is written first in the formula. The ionic charges must balance, and the ions must be combined in the lowest whole-number ratio.

② Solve **Apply the concepts to this situation.**

Write the symbol and charge for each ion, with the cation first.

The ions are _____ and _____.

Fill in the charges in the crisscross diagram to begin writing the formula for the compound. Then complete the formula by adding the subscripts for each element.

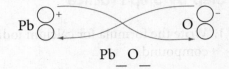

Pb _ O _

Reduce subscripts to the lowest whole-number ratio. The subscripts 2 and 4 can both be divided by 2. The ratio 2:4 is the same as the ratio 1:2. Write the formula with the smaller ratio.

The simplified formula is _____

Check that the ionic charges add up to zero.

_____ × (+4) + _____ × (−2) = _____

On Your Own

3. The compound gallium(III) oxide is used in semiconductors and lasers. Write the formula for this compound.

_____

4. Zirconium(IV) fluoride is used in glass for fiber optic sensors. Write the formula for this ionic compound.

_____

5. Write the chemical formula of barium nitride.

_____

6. Write the formula for tungsten(VI) oxide.

_____

More Practice Naming Binary Ionic Compounds   Lesson 9.2

Step-by-Step Practice

1. Name the binary ionic compound Cr_2O_3.

❶ Analyze **Identify the relevant concepts.**

The ions in a binary ionic compound are named in the order in which they appear in the formula. The cation is first, followed by the anion. Check to see if a metal ion has more than one possible ionic charge. If it does, include a Roman numeral after the cation name to indicate the charge.

❷ Solve **Apply the concepts to this situation.**

Identify the elements listed in the formula. Cr_2O_3 contains chromium and oxygen.

Oxygen forms anions. The name of the anion needs to end in –*ide*. Write the name of the anion.   Oxygen forms oxide anions.

Chromium atoms can lose either two or three electrons. List the possible cations that can form. Cr^{2+} and Cr^{3+}

Use the subscripts in the formula and the charge of the anion to find the charge of the cation. The oxide anion has a charge of -2 and that is the subscript for the Cr, so by the crisscross method, the chromium ion must have a $+3$ charge.

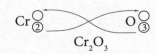

Write the name of the cation, followed by a Roman numeral. Add the name of the anion.   chromium(III) oxide

....

2. Write the name of the binary ionic compound Mg_3P_2.

❶ Analyze **Identify the relevant concepts.**

Name the ions in the order they appear in the formula—the cation and then the anion. Check to see if the metal ion has more than one possible ionic charge.

❷ Solve **Apply the concepts to this situation.**

Identify the elements listed in the formula. Mg_3P_2 contains _____ atoms and _____ atoms.

Write the name of the anion.   The anion is _____

| What charge does a magnesium ion have? | Magnesium ions have a _____ charge. |

| Is a Roman numeral needed in the name? Circle the correct answer. | No Yes |

| Write the name of the cation, followed by the name of the anion. | The name of the compound is _____ |

On Your Own

3. Li_2S is a compound that has a rotten egg odor. Name the compound whose formula is Li_2S.

_____

_____

4. Name the compound Re_2O_5. Use a Roman numeral after the name of the cation.

_____

_____

5. The compound MnF_3 is a purple colored solid that melts at temperatures greater than 600°C. Manganese can have more than one possible ionic charge. Name the compound whose formula is MnF_3.

_____

More Practice Naming Binary Molecular Compounds Lesson 9.3

Step-by-Step Practice

1. Name the molecular compound P_2S_5.

   ❶ **Analyze** Identify the relevant concepts.

   Name the elements in the order in which they are written in the formula. Use prefixes to show the number of atoms of an element. Use the ending *-ide* in the name of the second element.

   ❷ **Solve** Apply the concepts to this situation.

Identify the elements in the compound.	phosphorus and sulfur
Write the names of both elements. Remember to use the ending *-ide* at the end of the name of the second element.	phosphorus sulfide
Identify the number of atoms of each element in the formula.	2 phosphorus atoms 5 sulfur atoms
Add a prefix to the first name to show the number of atoms of phosphorus. The prefix *di-* is used to show 2.	diphosphorus sulfide
Add the prefix *penta-* to show that there are five atoms of sulfur.	diphosphorus pentasulfide
Write the complete name of the compound.	diphosphorus pentasulfide

2. Name the compound Cl_2O_6.

   ❶ **Analyze** Identify the relevant concepts.

   Name the elements in the formula and use prefixes to show the number of atoms of each element.

   ❷ **Solve** Apply the concepts to this situation.

Identify the elements in the compound and the number of atoms of each.	2 _____ atoms 6 _____ atoms
Write the names of the elements and add prefixes to show the number of atoms of each. Use the prefix *hex-* for 6. Use the ending *-ide* in the name of the second element.	The name of Cl_2O_6 is _____

On Your Own

3. Name the compound with the formula S_2Br_2.

_____

4. One of the compounds used to make superconductors is CSe_2. What is the name of this compound?

_____

5. The compound BrF_5 is an ingredient in liquid rocket propellants. Write the name of the compound BrF_5.

_____

6. Write the name of the compound N_4Se_4. *Hint:* Use the prefix *tetra-* for 4.

_____

9 Standardized Test Prep Tutor

The lettered choices below refer to Questions 7–10. You will be shown how to solve Questions 7 and 8. Then you will solve Questions 9 and 10 on your own.

    (A) QR   **(C)** Q_2R

    (B) QR_2 **(D)** Q_2R_3

Which formula shows the correct ratio of ions in the compound formed by each pair of elements?

	Element Q	**Element R**
7.	aluminum	sulfur
8.	potassium	oxygen
9.	lithium	chlorine
10.	strontium	bromine

7. Aluminum belongs to Group 3A. Aluminum will lose 3 electrons.

Use a criss cross diagram to find the formula. Even without identifying the charge of S, you know that the formula will have a subscript of 3 on the second element.

There is only one answer that has a subscript of 3.

Al^{3+} will be the ion formed.

The correct answer is D.

8. Potassium belongs to Group 1A. Potassium will lose one electron.

Set up a criss cross diagram and fill in the charge of potassium. Answers A or C would match with the formula so far. You will need to determine the charge of the oxygen ion to eliminate one of those answers.

Oxygen belongs to Group 6A. Oxygen will gain 2 electrons.

Potassium will form the ion K^+.

Oxygen will form the ion O^{2-}.

Find the answer that matches the formula.

The correct answer is C.

Now you try it.

9. Which formula shows the correct ratio of ions in the compound formed by lithium and chlorine?

10. Which formula shows the correct ratio of ions in the compound formed by strontium and bromine?

Use the data table to answer Questions 11–12. The table gives formulas for some of the ionic compounds formed when cations (M, N, P) combine with anions (A, B, C, D). Some formulas have been replaced by numbers.

Cation	Anion			
	A	B	C	D
M	MA_2	(1)	(2)	MD
N	(3)	N_2B	(4)	(5)
P	PA_3	(6)	PC	P_2D_3

11. Use the given formulas to determine the ionic charge of each cation and anion.

Look at the formula MA_2. Use a criss cross diagram to determine the charges of the ions.

Use the charge for A and the formula PA_3 to find the charge on P.

Use the charge for P and the formula P_2D_3 to find the charge on D.

Look at the formula PC. The charge of C needs to balance the charge of P in a 1:1 ratio.

Now you try it.

Use the formula N_2B to find the charges of B and N.

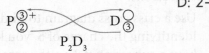

M: 2+

A: 1−

P: 3+

D: 2−

C: 3−

B: ____   N: ____

12. Write formulas for compounds (1) through (6).

The table summarizes the charges for ions A, C, D, M, and P. Add the charges for B and N. Then use the charges to find the missing formulas.

Cation	Anion			
	A^{1-}	B	C^{3-}	D^{2-}
M^{2+}	MA_2	(1)	(2)	MD
N	(3)	N_2B	(4)	(5)
P^{3+}	PA_3	(6)	PC	P_2D_3

Formula (1) = _____

Formula (2) = _____

Formula (3) = _____

Formula (4) = _____

Formula (5) = _____

Formula (6) = _____

More Practice Finding Mass from a Count

Step-by-Step Practice

1. What is the mass of 90 apples if one dozen apples have a mass of 2.0 kg?

❶ **Analyze** List the knowns and the unknown.

Knowns	Unknown
number of apples = 90 apples	mass of 90 apples = ? kg
12 apples = 1 dozen apples	
1 dozen apples = 2.0 kg apples	

❷ **Calculate** Solve for the unknown.

First, identify the sequence of conversions needed to do the calculation.

number of apples ⟶ dozens of apples ⟶ mass of apples

Write the conversion factor that can be used to convert from number of apples to dozens of apples.

$$\frac{1 \text{ dozen apples}}{12 \text{ apples}}$$

Write the factor that can be used to convert from dozens of apples to mass of apples.

$$\frac{2.0 \text{ kg}}{1 \text{ dozen apples}}$$

Multiply the number of apples by the two conversion factors.

$$90 \text{ apples} \times \frac{1 \text{ dozen apples}}{12 \text{ apples}} \times \frac{2.0 \text{ kg}}{1 \text{ dozen apples}}$$

$$= 15 \text{ kg}$$

❸ **Evaluate** Does the result make sense?

A dozen apples has a mass of 2.0 kg and 90 apples is less than 10 dozen apples. So it makes sense that the mass is less than 20 kg (10 dozen × 2.0 kg per dozen).

2. If 0.20 bushel is one dozen apples, and the mass of one dozen apples is 2.0 kg, what is the mass of 0.50 bushel?

① Analyze List the knowns and the unknown.

Knowns	Unknown
bushels of apples = 0.50 bushel	mass of 0.50 bushel of apples = ? kg
0.20 bushel of apples = 1 dozen apples	
1 dozen apples = 2.0 kg apples	

② Calculate Solve for the unknown.

Identify the sequence of conversions needed to do the calculation.

bushels of apples ⟶ _____ of apples ⟶ _____ of apples

Write the factor to convert from bushels of apples to dozens of apples. Then write the factor that can be used to convert from dozens of apples to mass of apples.

$$\frac{1 \text{ dozen apples}}{} \qquad \frac{}{1 \text{ dozen apples}}$$

Multiply the bushels of apples by the two conversion factors.

$$0.50 \text{ bushel of apples} \times \frac{1 \text{ dozen apples}}{}$$

$$\times \frac{}{1 \text{ dozen apples}} =$$

③ Evaluate Does the result make sense?

_____

_____

On Your Own

3. If an apple has eight seeds, and one apple has a mass of 0.2 kg, how many apple seeds are in 14 kg of apples?

4. A case of paper has a mass of 2000 g. A case of paper contains 10 reams of paper. One ream of paper is 500 sheets. What is the mass, in grams, of 50 sheets of paper?
Hint: You will need three conversion factors.

Interpret Data Mass Ratio of Carbon to Hydrogen Lesson 10.1

Preview the Table

Carbon Atoms		Hydrogen Atoms		Mass Ratio
Number	Mass (amu)	Number	Mass (amu)	$\dfrac{\text{Mass carbon}}{\text{Mass hydrogen}}$
●	12	●	1	$\dfrac{12 \text{ amu}}{1 \text{ amu}} = \dfrac{12}{1}$
● ●	24 (2 × 12)	● ●	2 (2 × 1)	$\dfrac{24 \text{ amu}}{2 \text{ amu}} = \dfrac{12}{1}$
●●●●● ●●●●●	120 (10 × 12)	●●●●● ●●●●●	10 (10 × 1)	$\dfrac{120 \text{ amu}}{10 \text{ amu}} = \dfrac{12}{1}$
●●●●●●●●●● ●●●●●●●●●● ●●●●●●●●●● ●●●●●●●●●● ●●●●●●●●●●	600 (50 × 12)	●●●●●●●●●● ●●●●●●●●●● ●●●●●●●●●● ●●●●●●●●●● ●●●●●●●●●●	50 (50 × 1)	$\dfrac{600 \text{ amu}}{50 \text{ amu}} = \dfrac{12}{1}$
Avogadro's number	$(6.02 \times 10^{23}) \times (12)$	Avogadro's number	$(6.02 \times 10^{23}) \times (1)$	$\dfrac{(6.02 \times 10^{23}) \times (12)}{(6.02 \times 10^{23}) \times (1)} = \dfrac{12}{1}$

This table compares the mass of carbon atoms to the mass of hydrogen atoms. The unit of mass is the atomic mass unit (amu). Remember that an amu is one-twelfth the mass of a carbon-12 atom.

Look at the first column. Dots are used to represent the number of carbon atoms in the first four rows. How many carbon atoms are in the fourth row?

_____

Look at the column labeled "Hydrogen Atoms." It looks a lot like the first column. One difference is the size of the dots representing the atoms. What is another difference?

_____

Look at the third column. Data from the first two columns is presented as a ratio. The mass of a given number of carbon atoms is the numerator of the ratio. The mass of the same number of hydrogen atoms is the denominator.

Analyze the Table

Now you are ready to answer some more questions. As you read the questions:

▶ Highlight key words.
▶ Circle numbers and units.

Use the first question as an example.

1. Read Tables What is the mass of 10 carbon atoms? What is the mass of 10 hydrogen atoms?

> Try it! Find the row that has 10 dots.

_____

2. Read Tables What is the mass ratio of 10 carbon atoms to 10 hydrogen atoms?

> Try it! Divide the mass of 10 carbon atoms by the mass of 10 hydrogen atoms.

_____

3. Calculate What is the mass of 25 carbon atoms? What is the mass of 25 hydrogen atoms?

> Try it! Multiply the mass of one atom (in amu) by the number of atoms.

_____

_____

On Your Own

4. Calculate What is the mass ratio of 25 carbon atoms to 25 hydrogen atoms?

_____

5. Read Tables What is the ratio when the number of carbon atoms is 6.02×10^{23} and the number of hydrogen atoms is 6.02×10^{23}?

_____

6. Make Generalizations What is the mass ratio of x number of carbon atoms to x number of hydrogen atoms? Give a reason for your answer.

_____

_____

7. Infer Do 36.0 kg of carbon atoms and 3.0 kg of hydrogen atoms have the same number of atoms? *Hint:* Divide the mass of carbon (36.0 kg) by the mass of hydrogen (3.0 kg).

_____

_____

More Practice Finding the Molar Mass of a Compound   Lesson 10.1

Step-by-Step Practice

1. What is the molar mass of hydrazine (N_2H_4)?

   ❶ **Analyze List the knowns and the unknown.**

Knowns	Unknown
chemical formula = N_2H_4	molar mass of N_2H_4 = ? g/mol
mass of 1 mol N = 14.0 g	
mass of 1 mol H = 1.0 g	

   ❷ **Calculate Solve for the unknown.**

   To find the molar mass of a compound, you need to sum the masses of the elements in the compound.

   Find the number of moles of N and H in 1 mol of N_2H_4.

   $$\frac{2 \text{ mol N atoms}}{4 \text{ mol H atoms}}$$

   Multiply the number of moles of each element by the molar mass of the element.

   $$2 \text{ mol N} \times \frac{14.0 \text{ g N}}{1 \text{ mol N}} = 28.0 \text{ g N}$$

   $$4 \text{ mol H} \times \frac{1.0 \text{ g H}}{1 \text{ mol H}} = 4.0 \text{ g H}$$

   Find the sum of the masses.

   mass of 1 mol N_2H_4 = 28.0 g N + 4.0 g H = 32.0 g

   molar mass of N_2H_4 = 32.0 g/mol

   ❸ **Evaluate Does the result make sense?**

   Check the math without the units to make sure your answer makes sense. $2 \times 14 + 4 \times 1 = 28 + 4 = 32$. Yes, the answers match.

2. Calcium chloride ($CaCl_2$) is used to de-ice roadways and sidewalks. Calculate the molar mass of this compound.

   ❶ **Analyze List the knowns and the unknown.**

Knowns	Unknown
chemical formula = $CaCl_2$	molar mass of $CaCl_2$ = ? g/mol
mass of 1 mol Ca = _____	
mass of 1 mol Cl = _____	

❷ Calculate Solve for the unknown.

Find the number of moles of Ca and Cl in
1 mol of $CaCl_2$.

_____ mol Ca atoms

_____ mol Cl atoms

Multiply the number of moles of each element
by the molar mass of that element.

_____ ~~mol Ca~~ $\times \dfrac{}{1~\text{mol Ca}}$ = _____ g Ca

_____ ~~mol Cl~~ $\times \dfrac{}{}$ = _____ g Cl

Find the total mass of the compound.

mass of 1 mol $CaCl_2$ = _____ g Ca + _____ g Cl

= _____ g

molar mass $CaCl_2$ = _____ g

❸ Evaluate Does the result make sense?

_____

_____

On Your Own

3. The compound aluminum selenide (Al_2Se_3) is used to make semiconductors. Calculate
the molar mass of aluminum selenide.

4. Table sugar, or sucrose, has the formula $C_{12}H_{22}O_{11}$. Calculate the molar mass of this
molecule.

More Practice Converting Between Moles and Mass   Lesson 10.2

Step-by-Step Practice

1. What is the mass, in grams, of 0.250 mol K_2CO_3?

➊ **Analyze** List the known and the unknown.

Known	Unknown
number of moles of K_2CO_3 = 0.250 mol	mass = ? g K_2CO_3

➋ **Calculate** Solve for the unknown.

Use the molar mass of the compound as a conversion factor to convert from moles to mass.

First, find the mass of 1 mol of K_2CO_3. The mass is the sum of the masses of the individual elements.

One mole K_2CO_3 is made of:

2 mol K atoms

1 mol C atoms

3 mol O atoms.

$$2 \text{ mol K} \times \frac{39.1 \text{ g K}}{1 \text{ mol K}} = 78.2 \text{ g K}$$

$$1 \text{ mol C} \times \frac{12.0 \text{ g C}}{1 \text{ mol C}} = 12.0 \text{ g C}$$

$$3 \text{ mol O} \times \frac{16.0 \text{ g O}}{1 \text{ mol O}} = 48.0 \text{ g O}$$

$$1 \text{ mol } K_2CO_3 = 78.2 \text{ g K} + 12.0 \text{ g C} + 48.0 \text{ g O}$$
$$= 138.2 \text{ g } K_2CO_3$$

Multiply the number of moles to be converted by the molar mass.

$$0.250 \text{ mol } K_2CO_3 \times \frac{138.2 \text{ g } K_2CO_3}{1 \text{ mol } K_2CO_3}$$
$$= 34.6 \text{ g } K_2CO_3$$

➌ **Evaluate** Does the result make sense?

The molar mass of K_2CO_3 is about 140 g/mol. The value to be converted is 0.250 mol, or 1/4 of a mol. So 1/4 × 140 g is about 35 g. The answer 34.6 g makes sense.

....

2. How many moles are in 20.0 g of sulfur tetroxide?

➊ **Analyze** List the known and the unknown.

Known	Unknown
mass of SO_4 = _____ g	number of moles SO_4 = ? mol SO_4

❷ Calculate Solve for the unknown.

Use the molar mass of the compound as a conversion factor.

Determine the molar mass of SO_4.

1 mol SO_4 = _____ mol S + _____ mol O

$$\_\_\_\_ \text{ mol S} \times \frac{32.1 \text{ g S}}{1 \text{ mol S}} = _____ \text{ S}$$

$$\_\_\_\_ \text{ mol O} \times \frac{16.0 \text{ g O}}{1 \text{ mol O}} = \_\_\_\_\_ \text{ O}$$

1 mol SO_4 = _____ g S + _____ g O = _____ SO_4

Use the molar mass to convert from mass of SO_4 to moles.

_____ g SO_4 × ————— = _____ SO_4

❸ Evaluate Does the result make sense?

The molar mass of sulfur tetroxide is about 100 g/mol. The value to be converted is 20.0 g, which is 1/5 of the molar mass. 1/5 = 0.2. Is the calculated value of moles of sulfate the same fraction? _____

On Your Own

3. What is the mass of 2.50 mol of methane (CH_4)?

4. The compound phenol (C_6H_6O) was used as an antiseptic because it kills germs quickly. How many moles are in 83.0 g of phenol?

More Practice Calculating Percent Composition

Lesson 10.3

Step-by-Step Practice

1. A 10.0 g sample of a compound made of aluminum and selenium contains 8.0 g of selenium. What is the percent composition of this compound?

   ❶ Analyze List the knowns and the unknowns.

Knowns	Unknowns
mass of compound = 10.0 g	percent by mass of Se = ?% Se
mass of selenium in compound = 8.0 g	percent by mass of Al = ?% Al

   ❷ Calculate Solve for the unknown.

   Divide the mass of the element by the mass of the compound. Then multiply by 100%.

   The compound has a mass of 10.0 g. The selenium in the compound has a mass of 8.0 g. Subtract to find the mass of aluminum in the compound.

   mass of Al = mass of compound − mass of Se
   mass of Al = 10.0 g compound − 8.0 g Se
   mass of Al = 2.0 g Al

   Write and solve the equation for percent by mass for each element in the compound.

   % by mass of element = $\dfrac{\text{mass of element}}{\text{mass of compound}} \times 100\%$

   $\%\text{Se} = \dfrac{8.0\ g}{10.0\ g} \times 100\% = \boxed{80.0\%\ \text{Se}}$

   $\%\text{Al} = \dfrac{2.0\ g}{10.0\ g} \times 100\% = \boxed{20.0\%\ \text{Al}}$

   ❸ Evaluate Does the result make sense?

   The mass of the selenium is more than half of the total mass, so it makes sense that the percentage would be greater than 50 percent.

   ....

2. Zinc carbonate ($ZnCO_3$) is used as a zinc supplement in animal feed. What is the percent composition of zinc carbonate?

   ❶ Analyze List the known and the unknowns.

Known	Unknowns
chemical formula = $ZnCO_3$	percent by mass of Zn = ?% Zn
	percent by mass of C = ?% C
	percent by mass of O = ?% O

❷ Calculate **Solve for the unknown.**

Divide the mass of the element by the total molar mass
of the compound. Then multiply by 100%.

Determine the molar mass of $ZnCO_3$.

$$1 \text{ mol } ZnCO_3 = \text{\_\_\_\_\_ g Zn} + \text{\_\_\_\_\_ g C} + \text{\_\_\_\_\_ g O}$$

$$= \text{\_\_\_\_\_ g } ZnCO_3$$

$$1 \text{ mol Zn} \times \frac{65.4 \text{ g Zn}}{1 \text{ mol Zn}} = \text{_____}$$

$$1 \text{ mol C} \times \frac{12.0 \text{ g C}}{1 \text{ mol C}} = \text{_____}$$

$$3 \text{ mol O} \times \frac{16.0 \text{ g O}}{1 \text{ mol O}} = \text{_____}$$

Determine the percent by mass of zinc.

$$\% \text{ Zn} = \frac{\text{mass of Zn in 1 mol of } ZnCO_3}{\text{molar mass } ZnCO_3}$$

$$\% \text{ Zn} = \frac{65.4 \text{ g}}{125.4 \text{ g}} \times 100\% = \text{\_\_\_\_\_}\% \text{ Zn}$$

Determine the percent by mass of carbon and oxygen.

$$\% \text{ C} = \frac{\text{mass of C in 1 mol of } ZnCO_3}{\text{molar mass } ZnCO_3}$$

$$\% \text{ O} = \frac{\text{mass of O in 1 mol of } ZnCO_3}{\text{molar mass } ZnCO_3}$$

$$\% \text{ C} = \frac{}{125.4 \text{ g}} \times 100\% = \text{_____}$$

$$\% \text{ O} = \frac{}{\text{_____}} \times 100\% = \text{_____}$$

❸ Evaluate **Does the result make sense?**

Make sure that the percentages add up to about 100%:

_____% + _____% + _____% = _____%.

On Your Own

3. A 2.5 g sample of a potassium and bromine compound contains 0.75 g K and 1.75 g Br.
What is the percent composition of each element in this compound?

4. A 40.0 g sample of ore contains 18.0 g Fe and the rest of the mass is oxygen. What is the
percent composition of this sample? *Hint:* Subtract the mass of Fe from the total mass to
find the mass of oxygen.

10 Standardized Test Prep Tutor

Read the question. The highlighted words tell you what property the correct nitrogen compound will have.

5. Which of these compounds has the largest percent by mass of nitrogen?

    (A) N_2O (D) N_2O_3

    (B) NO   (E) N_2O_4

    (C) NO_4

❶ Analyze

You could calculate the molar mass of each compound and then figure out what percent of the mass is nitrogen. But for this problem, there is a shortcut. Because the same two elements are in each compound, you only need to find the compound that has the greatest ratio of nitrogen to oxygen.

❷ Solve

The ratios are based on the number of atoms of nitrogen and oxygen in a molecule of the compound.

The ratio of nitrogen to oxygen in answer A is 2:1.

The ratio of nitrogen to oxygen in answer B is 1:1.

The ratio of nitrogen to oxygen in answer C is 1:4.

What is the ratio of nitrogen to oxygen in answer D?   D = _____

What is the ratio of nitrogen to oxygen in answer E?   E = _____

❸ Choose an Answer

Which compound has the greatest ratio of nitrogen to oxygen? The correct answer is A.

Now you try it.

Which of these compounds has the largest percent by mass of oxygen?

(A) MnO   (D) Mn_2O_7

(B) MnO_2 (E) Mn_3O_4

(C) Mn_2O_3

Read the question. The highlighted phrase tells what you are looking for.

7. Allicin ($C_6H_{10}S_2O$) is the compound that gives garlic its odor. A sample of allicin contains 3.0×10^{21} atoms of carbon. How many hydrogen atoms does this sample contain?

(A) 10   (C) 1.8×10^{21}

(B) 1.0×10^{21} (D) 5.0×10^{21}

❶ Analyze

Use the ratio of hydrogen to carbon atoms in the formula. For every 10 atoms of hydrogen in $C_6H_{10}S_2O$, there are 6 atoms of carbon. The ratio of hydrogen atoms to carbon atoms is 10:6, or 5:3.

❷ Solve

Multiply the number of carbon atoms by the ratio.

$$3.0 \times 10^{21} \text{ C atoms} \times \frac{5 \text{ H atoms}}{3 \text{ C atoms}}$$
$$= 5.0 \times 10^{21} \text{ H atoms}$$

❸ Choose an Answer

Look at the answer choices. Find the choice that matches the calculation. The correct answer is D.

Now you try it.

A sample of calcium carbonate, $CaCO_3$, contains 1.4×10^{19} atoms of carbon. How many oxygen atoms does this sample contain?

(A) 1.4×10^{19} (C) 4.2×10^{19}

(B) 2.8×10^{19} (D) 8.4×10^{19}

A sample of NH_4NO_3 contains 4.0×10^{25} atoms of nitrogen. How many hydrogen atoms does this sample contain?

(A) 4.0×10^{25} (C) 8.0×10^{25}

(B) 2.0×10^{25} (D) 1.0×10^{26}

More Practice Writing and Balancing Equations   Lesson 11.1

Step-by-Step Practice

1. When solid barium oxide and aluminum are heated to a high temperature, the products are liquid barium and solid aluminum oxide.

   ❶ **Analyze** Identify the relevant concepts.

   Identify the reactants and products and write a formula for each one. Write a skeleton equation for the reaction. Use coefficients to balance the equation.

   ❷ **Solve** Apply the concepts to this problem.

   Write a formula for each reactant and product.

Reactants	Products
BaO(s)	Ba(l)
Al(s)	Al$_2$O$_3$(s)

   Write a skeleton equation for the reaction. Check to see if the equation is balanced as written. It is not balanced because there are more aluminum and oxygen atoms on the right side of the equation than on the left.

   $$BaO(s) + Al(s) \longrightarrow Ba(l) + Al_2O_3(s)$$

   Add coefficients to the reactants to balance aluminum and oxygen.

   $$3BaO(s) + 2Al(s) \longrightarrow Ba(l) + Al_2O_3(s)$$

   Now there are more barium atoms on the left than on the right. Add a coefficient in front of Ba(l) to finish balancing the equation.

   $$3BaO(s) + 2Al(s) \longrightarrow 3Ba(l) + Al_2O_3(s)$$

2. When boron oxide (B$_2$O$_3$) reacts with magnesium, the products are boron and magnesium oxide. The reactants and products are solids.

   ❶ **Analyze** Identify the relevant concepts.

   Write a skeleton equation for the reaction. Use coefficients to balance the equation.

❷ Solve **Apply the concepts to this problem.**

Write a formula for each reactant and product.

Reactants	Products
BaO(s)	B(s)
Mg(s)	MgO(s)

Write a skeleton equation for the reaction. $B_2O_3(s) + Mg(s) \longrightarrow B(s) + MgO(s)$

Explain why the equation is not balanced as written.

_____

_____

Add coefficients to balance the equation. $B_2O_3(s) + \underline{\hspace{1cm}} Mg(s) \longrightarrow \underline{\hspace{1cm}} B(s) + \underline{\hspace{1cm}} MgO(s)$

On Your Own

3. Zinc metal reacts with oxygen to form solid zinc(II) oxide. Write a balanced equation for this reaction.

4. When solid mercury oxide(II) is heated, liquid mercury and oxygen gas are produced. Write a balanced equation for this reaction.

5. Chlorine gas is bubbled into a solution of potassium iodide. The products of the reaction are aqueous potassium chloride and solid iodine (I_2). Write a balanced equation for this reaction.

More Practice

Combination and Decomposition Reactions

Step-by-Step Practice

1. Write a balanced equation for the combination of potassium and chlorine.

$$K(s) + Cl_2(g) \longrightarrow$$

❶ Analyze Identify the relevant concepts.

Potassium is in Group 1A on the periodic table. Chlorine is in Group 7A.

❷ Solve Apply the concepts to this problem.

Identify the binary ionic compound that can be formed by the combination of potassium and chlorine. This compound is potassium chloride. Write the symbol and charge for each ion in the compound. Then write the formula for the product.

Ions	Product
K^+	KCl
Cl^-	

Write a skeleton equation for the reaction. Check to see if the equation is balanced as written. It is not balanced because there are more chlorine atoms on the left side of the equation than on the right.

$$K(s) + Cl_2(g) \longrightarrow KCl(s)$$

Add a coefficient to the product to balance chlorine.

$$K(s) + Cl_2(g) \longrightarrow 2KCl(s)$$

Now there are more potassium atoms on the right side than on the left side. Add a coefficient in front of $K(s)$ to finish balancing the equation.

$$2K(s) + Cl_2(g) \longrightarrow 2KCl(s)$$

2. Write a balanced equation for the decomposition of aluminum chloride.

$$AlCl_3(s) \longrightarrow$$

❶ Analyze Identify the relevant concepts.

The elements that make up aluminum chloride are aluminum and chlorine. Aluminum is a solid. Chlorine is a gas that is found as a diatomic molecule.

❷ Solve **Apply the concepts to this problem.**

Write the formula for each product.

Products
_____
_____

Write a skeleton equation for the reaction.

$$AlCl_3(s) \longrightarrow Al(s) + Cl_2(g)$$

Explain why the equation is not balanced as written.

_____

_____

Add coefficients to balance the equation.

$$\_\_\_ AlCl_3(s) \longrightarrow$$
$$\_\_\_ Al(s) + \_\_\_ Cl_2(g)$$

On Your Own

3. Chromium(III) oxide (Cr_2O_3) is a solid compound that is used in some paints. Complete the decomposition equation for the reaction. Then balance the equation.

$$Cr_2O_3(s) \longrightarrow$$

4. Lithium phosphide (Li_3P) is a compound used in the production of lasers for barcode scanners. Write and balance an equation for the combination of lithium and phosphorous solids that produces lithium phosphide gas.

5. Write and balance the equation for the combination reaction that produces solid gold(III) chloride ($AuCl_3$) from solid gold and chlorine gas.

More Practice Replacement Reactions

Step-by-Step Practice

1. Write a balanced equation for the following single-replacement reaction.

$$Na(s) + ZnI_2(aq) \longrightarrow$$

❶ Analyze **Identify the relevant concepts.**

Determine whether a replacement reaction can happen. If it can, write a skeleton equation for the reaction. Use coefficients to balance the equation.

❷ Calculate **Apply the concepts to this problem.**

Determine whether the reaction will take place. Sodium is more reactive than zinc. That means sodium will replace zinc in its compounds. So a reaction will take place.

Write a skeleton equation for the reaction. Check to see if the equation is balanced as written. It is not balanced because there are more iodine atoms on the left side of the equation than on the right side.

$$Na(s) + ZnI_2(aq) \longrightarrow NaI(aq) + Zn(s)$$

Add a coefficient to NaI(aq) to balance iodine.

$$Na(s) + ZnI_2(aq) \longrightarrow 2NaI(aq) + Zn(s)$$

Now there are more sodium atoms on the right side than on the left. Add a coefficient in front of Na(s) to finish balancing the equation.

$$2Na(s) + ZnI_2(aq) \longrightarrow 2NaI(aq) + Zn(s)$$

. . . .

2. A precipitate of copper hydroxide, $Cu(OH)_2$, forms when an aqueous solution of copper chloride, $CuCl_2$, reacts with an aqueous solution of aluminum hydroxide, $Al(OH)_3$. Write a balanced chemical equation for the double-replacement reaction.

$$CuCl_2(aq) + Al(OH)_3(aq) \longrightarrow$$

❶ Analyze **Identify the relevant concepts.**

Write a skeleton equation for the reaction. Include a solid precipitate as one of the products. Use coefficients to balance the equation.

❷ Solve **Apply the concepts to this problem.**

Write a skeleton equation for the reaction.

$$CuCl_2(aq) + Al(OH)_3(aq) \longrightarrow$$
$$Cu(OH)_2(s) + AlCl_3(aq)$$

Explain why the equation is not balanced as written.

_____

_____

_____

Add coefficients to balance the Cl^- and OH^- ions.

_____$CuCl_2(aq)$ + _____$Al(OH)_3(aq)$ $\longrightarrow$

_____$Cu(OH)_2(s)$ + _____$AlCl_3(aq)$

On Your Own

3. Solid boron nitride reacts in fluorine gas to form solid boron trifluoride (BF_3) and nitrogen gas. Complete and balance the equation for this single-replacement reaction.

$BN(s) + F_2(g) \longrightarrow$

4. Chlorine gas is bubbled through an aqueous solution of potassium iodide. These substances react to form an aqueous solution of potassium chloride and solid iodine. Complete and balance the equation for this single-replacement reaction.

$KI(aq) + Cl_2(g) \longrightarrow$

5. Complete and balance the equation for this double-replacement reaction. *Hint:* The product containing calcium ions is a solid.

$Ca(OH)_2(aq) + NH_4Cl(aq) \longrightarrow$

More Practice Net Ionic Equations

Step-by-Step Practice

1. Aqueous solutions of aluminum nitrate, $Al(NO_3)_3$, and sodium hydroxide, NaOH, are mixed. A precipitate of aluminum hydroxide, $Al(OH)_3$, forms. Write a balanced net ionic equation for the reaction.

> **❶ Analyze** Identify the relevant concepts.
>
> Write the complete ionic equation. Eliminate ions that appear as both reactants and products. Then balance the equation with respect to both mass and charge.

> **❷ Calculate** Apply the concepts to this problem.

Write a skeleton equation for the reaction.	$Al(NO_3)_3(aq) + NaOH(aq) \longrightarrow$ $Al(OH)_3(s) + NaNO_3(aq)$
Write the complete ionic equation for the reaction. Show any ionic compounds that are dissolved in solution as individual ions. Balance the ions as needed.	$Al^{3+}(aq) + 3NO_3^-(aq) + 3Na^+(aq) + 3OH^-(aq) \longrightarrow$ $Al(OH)_3(s) + 3Na^+(aq) + 3NO_3^-(aq)$
Eliminate ions that appear as both reactants and products. These spectator ions are NO_3^- and Na^+.	$Al^{3+}(aq) + \cancel{3NO_3^-}(aq) + \cancel{3Na^+}(aq) + 3OH^-(aq) \longrightarrow$ $Al(OH)_3(s) + \cancel{3Na^+}(aq) + \cancel{3NO_3^-}(aq)$
Write the net ionic equation. Make sure the atoms and charges in the equation are balanced.	$Al^{3+}(aq) + 3OH^-(aq) \longrightarrow Al(OH)_3(s)$

....

2. Aqueous solutions of lithium sulfide, Li_2S, and nickel(II) nitrate, $Ni(NO_3)_2$, are mixed. A precipitate of nickel sulfide, NiS, forms. Write a balanced net ionic equation for the reaction.

> **❶ Analyze** Identify the relevant concepts.
>
> Write the complete ionic equation. Eliminate spectator ions. Then balance the equation with respect to both mass and charge.

> **❷ Calculate** Apply the concepts to this problem.

Write a skeleton equation for the reaction.	$Li_2S(aq) + Ni(NO_3)_2(aq) \longrightarrow$ _____ $(aq) +$ ____ (s)

Write the complete ionic equation for the reaction. Show any ionic compounds that are dissolved in solution as individual ions. Balance the ions as needed.

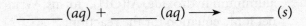

$2Li^+(aq) + S^{2-}(aq) + Ni^{2+}(aq) + 2NO_3^-(aq) \longrightarrow$

_____ (aq) + _____ (aq) + _____ (s)

Identify the spectator ions.

The spectator ions are _____ and _____.

Write the net ionic equation. Make sure the atoms and charges in the equation are balanced.

_____ (aq) + _____ (aq) $\longrightarrow$ _____ (s)

On Your Own

3. Write a balanced net ionic equation for the following reaction:

$Pb(NO_3)_2(aq) + 2KCl(aq) \longrightarrow PbCl_2(s) + 2KNO_3(aq)$

4. Aqueous solutions of sodium carbonate, Na_2CO_3, and iron(II) sulfate, $FeSO_4$, react. The reaction produces the precipitate iron(II) carbonate, $FeCO_3$.

a. What is the complete ionic equation for the reaction?

b. What is the net ionic equation?

c. What are the spectator ions?

11 Standardized Test Prep Tutor

Read the question. The highlighted term tells you what you need to find.

3. Magnesium ribbon reacts with an aqueous solution of copper(II) chloride in a single-replacement reaction. Which are the <mark>products of the balanced net ionic equation</mark> for the reaction?

(A) $Mg^{2+}(aq) + 2Cl^-(aq) + Cu(s)$
(B) $Mg^+(aq) + Cl^-(aq) + Cu^+(aq)$
(C) $Mg^{2+}(aq) + Cu(s)$
(D) $Cu(s) + 2Cl^-(aq)$

❶ Analyze

Write the balanced equation for the reaction.

$$Mg(s) + CuCl_2(aq) \longrightarrow$$
$$MgCl_2(aq) + Cu(s)$$

Use the balanced equation to write the complete ionic equation. Show soluble ionic compounds as individual ions.

$$Mg(s) + Cu^{2+}(aq) + 2Cl^-(aq) \longrightarrow$$
$$Mg^{2+}(aq) + 2Cl^-(aq) + Cu(s)$$

❷ Solve

A net ionic equation shows only the ions that are directly involved in the chemical change. The Cl^- ion appears on both sides of the equation, so it is a spectator ion. Remove Cl^- to obtain the net ionic equation.

$$Mg(s) + Cu^{2+}(aq) \longrightarrow$$
$$\underline{\quad\quad}(aq) + \underline{\quad\quad}(s)$$

Make sure the positive charges on the reactant side are balanced by the negative charges on the product side. Since they are, the net ionic equation is balanced.

❸ Choose an Answer

Look at the answer choices. Find the choice that matches the products of the net ionic equation. The correct answer is C.

Now you try it.

Zinc metal reacts with an aqueous solution of iron(II) sulfate in a single-replacement reaction. Which are the products of the balanced net ionic equation for the reaction?

(A) $Zn^{2+}(aq) + SO_4^{2-}(aq) + Fe(s)$
(B) $Zn^{2+}(aq) + SO_4^{2-}(aq) + 2Fe^+(aq)$
(C) $Fe(s) + SO_4^{2-}(aq)$
(D) $Zn^{2+}(aq) + Fe(s)$

Use the following description and data table to answer Questions 4–6.

Dropper bottles labeled P, Q, and R contain one of three aqueous solutions: potassium carbonate, K_2CO_3; hydrochloric acid, HCl; and calcium nitrate, $Ca(NO_3)_2$. The table shows what happens when pairs of solutions are mixed.

Solution	P	Q	R
P	—	Precipitate	No reaction
Q	Precipitate	—	Gas forms.
R	No reaction	Gas forms.	—

4. Identify the contents of each dropper bottle.

   Identify the possible products of a double-replacement reaction between each combination of reactants. Products that are soluble do not produce a reaction.

   $$K_2CO_3(aq) + 2HCl(aq) \longrightarrow$$
   $$2KCl(aq) + H_2O(l) + CO_2(g)$$
   $$K_2CO_3(aq) + Ca(NO_3)_2(aq) \longrightarrow$$
   $$CaCO_3(s) + 2KNO_3(aq)$$
   $$Ca(NO_3)_2(aq) + 2HCl(aq) \longrightarrow$$
   no reaction

   Compare the products of the double-replacement reactions to the data table.

   Solutions P and Q must be $K_2CO_3(aq)$ and $Ca(NO_3)_2(aq)$ because they produce a precipitate.

   Solution P =

   Solution Q =

   Solutions P and R must be $Ca(NO_3)_2(aq)$ and HCl(aq) because they do not produce a reaction.

   Solution R =

   Solutions Q and R must be $K_2CO_3(aq)$ and HCl(aq) because they produce a gas.

5. Write the net ionic equation for the formation of the precipitate.

   Use the correct balanced equation from question 4 to write the complete balanced ionic equation.

   $$2K^+(aq) + CO_3^{2-}(aq) + Ca^{2+}(aq) +$$
   $$2NO_3^-(aq) \longrightarrow CaCO_3(s) +$$
   $$2K^+(aq) + 2NO_3^-(aq)$$

   Remove the spectator ions K^+ and NO_3^-.

   $$CO_3^{2-}(aq) + Ca^{2+}(aq) \longrightarrow CaCO_3(s)$$

   Now you try it.

6. Write the complete ionic equation for the formation of the gas.

More Practice Calculating Moles of a Product

Lesson 12.2

Step-by-Step Practice

1. How many moles of Ca_3N_2 are produced when 0.75 mol of calcium reacts with nitrogen?

   ❶ **Analyze** List the known and the unknown.

Known	Unknown
moles of calcium = 0.75 mol Ca	moles of Ca_3N_2 = ?

   ❷ **Calculate** Solve for the unknown.

   Write a balanced chemical equation using calcium and nitrogen as reactants.

   $$3Ca(s) + N_2(g) \longrightarrow Ca_3N_2(s)$$

   Use the coefficients of Ca and Ca_3N_2 to write a ratio of moles of Ca_3N_2 to moles of Ca.

   $$\frac{1 \text{ mol } Ca_3N_2}{3 \text{ mol } Ca}$$

   Multiply the given moles of Ca by the mole ratio. $\quad 0.75 \text{ mol Ca} \times \dfrac{1 \text{ mol } Ca_3N_2}{3 \text{ mol Ca}} = 0.25 \text{ mol } Ca_3N_2$

   ❸ **Evaluate** Does the result make sense?

   The mole ratio of Ca_3N_2 to Ca in the balanced equation is 1:3. So a ratio of 0.25 mol Ca_3N_2 to 0.75 mol Ca makes sense.

2. How many moles of $AuCl_3$ are produced when gold reacts with 0.42 mol of chlorine gas?

   ❶ **Analyze** List the known and the unknown.

Known	Unknown
moles of chlorine = _____	moles of $AuCl_3$ = ?

   ❷ **Calculate** Solve for the unknown.

   Write the balanced chemical equation.

   $$\_\_\_\_ Au(s) + \_\_\_\_ Cl_2(g) \longrightarrow \_\_\_\_ AuCl_3(s)$$

   Use the coefficients in the equation to write a ratio of moles Cl_2 to moles of $AuCl_3$.

   $$\frac{2 \text{ mol } AuCl_3}{\rule{2cm}{0.4pt}}$$

   Multiply the given moles of Cl_2 by the mole ratio.

   $$0.42 \text{ mol } Cl_2 \times \frac{\rule{2cm}{0.4pt}}{\rule{2cm}{0.4pt}} =$$

③ Evaluate Does the result make sense?

Is the mole ratio of $AuCl_3$ to Cl_2 in the equation the same as the mole ratio of $AuCl_3$ produced to the moles of Cl_2 that reacted? Explain.

_____

On Your Own

3. Heating calcium carbonate ($CaCO_3$) to a high temperature produces carbon dioxide and lime (CaO), which is used to make bricks. How many moles of lime are produced for each 0.75 mole of $CaCO_3$ that decomposes?

4. Air pollution can occur when nitrogen oxide (NO) from car exhaust systems reacts with oxygen in the air to produce the reddish-brown gas nitrogen dioxide (NO_2). How many moles of nitrogen dioxide are produced for each 0.85 mol of oxygen gas that reacts?

5. One of the reactions used in fireworks is the decomposition of potassium chlorate ($KClO_3$) into potassium chloride (KCl) and oxygen gas. How many moles of KCl and how many moles of O_2 are produced when 0.60 mol $KClO_3$ decomposes? *Hint:* Do a separate calculation for each unknown.

More Practice Calculate the Mass of a Product Lesson 12.2

Step-by-Step Practice

1. Calculate the number of grams of Mg_3N_2 produced by the reaction of 246.5 g of magnesium with an excess of nitrogen. The balanced equation is:

$$3Mg(s) + N_2(g) \longrightarrow Mg_3N_3(s)$$

❶ **Analyze** List the knowns and the unknown.

Knowns	Unknown
mass of Mg = 246.5 g Mg	mass of Mg_3N_2 = ?
molar mass of Mg = 24.3 g/mol	
molar mass of Mg_3N_2 = 100.9 g/mol	

❷ **Calculate** Solve for the unknown.

Identify the steps needed to convert mass of Mg to mass of Mg_3N_2.

g Mg $\longrightarrow$ mol Mg $\longrightarrow$ mol Mg_3N_2 $\longrightarrow$ g Mg_3N_2

Use the coefficients of Mg_3N_2 and Mg in the balanced equation to find the mole ratio.

$$\frac{1 \text{ mol } Mg_3N_2}{3 \text{ mol } Mg}$$

Start with the known mass of Mg. Use conversion factors to calculate the mass of Mg_3N_2.

$$246.5 \text{ g Mg} \times \frac{1 \text{ mol Mg}}{24.3 \text{ g Mg}} \times \frac{1 \text{ mol } Mg_3N_2}{3 \text{ mol Mg}} \times \frac{100.9 \text{ g } Mg_3N_2}{1 \text{ mol } Mg_3N_2}$$

$$= 341.2 \text{ g } Mg_3N_3$$

❸ **Evaluate** Does the result make sense?

You might expect the mass of Mg_3N_2 to be about four times the mass of Mg, or about 1000 g, because Mg_3N_2 has about four times the molar mass of Mg. However, only one mole of Mg_3N_2 is produced for every 3 moles of Mg. So a result of about 1/3 of 1000 g makes sense.

2. Find the number of grams of sodium chloride (NaCl) produced when 82.4 g of aluminum chloride ($AlCl_3$) reacts with it.

$$2AlCl_3(aq) + 3Na_2CO_3(aq) \longrightarrow Al_2(CO_3)_3(s) + 6NaCl(aq)$$

❶ Analyze List the knowns and the unknown.

Knowns	Unknown
mass of $AlCl_3$ = _____	mass of NaCl = ?
mole ratio = 6 mol NaCl /_____	
molar mass of $AlCl_3$ = _____	
molar mass of NaCl = _____	

❷ Calculate Solve for the unknown.

Identify the steps needed to convert mass of $AlCl_3$ to mass of NaCl.

$$g\ AlCl_3 \longrightarrow \text{_____} \longrightarrow \text{_____} \longrightarrow g\ NaCl$$

Start with the known mass of $AlCl_3$. Use conversion factors to calculate the mass of NaCl.

$$82.4\ g\ AlCl_3 \times \text{_____} \times \frac{6\ mol\ NaCl}{\text{_____}} \times \text{_____}$$

$$= \text{\_\_\_\_\_} g\ NaCl$$

❸ Evaluate Does the result make sense?

For each mole of $AlCl_3$, how many moles of NaCl are produced? _____

The molar mass of NaCl is about what fraction of the molar mass of $AlCl_3$? _____

Is the calculated mass of NaCl close to the mass of $AlCl_3$ × the moles of NaCl and the molar mass fraction? Explain.

_____

On Your Own

3. Crime scene investigators can make fingerprints more visible by spraying them with zinc chloride ($ZnCl_2$). This compound can be produced by the reaction of zinc with hydrochloric acid (HCl). How many grams of zinc chloride are produced when 15.4 g of zinc reacts with HCl? The balanced equation is:

$$Zn(s) + 2HCl(aq) \longrightarrow H_2(g) + ZnCl_2(aq)$$

4. The reaction of aluminum and magnetite (Fe_3O_4) produces iron and aluminum oxide (Al_2O_3) a compound used in toothpaste to polish teeth. Write the balanced equation for this reaction. Then determine how many grams of Al_2O_3 are produced by a reaction of 26.3 g of Fe_3O_4 with aluminum.

More Practice
Volume-Volume Stoichiometric Calculations

Step-by-Step Practice

1. Bromine and nitrogen combine to form nitrogen tribromide (NBr_3). How many liters of NBr_3 gas are produced when 6.85 L of bromine reacts with excess nitrogen? Assume conditions are at STP.

$$3Br_2(g) + N_2(g) \longrightarrow 2NBr_3(g)$$

❶ **Analyze** **List the knowns and the unknown.**

Knowns	Unknown
volume of bromine = 6.85 L Br_2	volume of nitrogen tribromide = ? L NBr_3

❷ **Calculate** **Solve for the unknown.**

Identify the steps needed to convert liters of Br_2 to liters of NBr_3.

$$L\ Br_2 \longrightarrow mol\ Br_2 \longrightarrow mol\ NBr_3 \longrightarrow L\ NBr_3$$

Use the coefficients of NBr_3 and Br_2 from the balanced equation to write a mole ratio.

$$\frac{2\ mol\ NBr_3}{3\ mol\ Br_2}$$

Use the known volume of Br_2 and the appropriate conversion factors to calculate the volume of NBr_3. The conversion factors need to be set up so that the units cancel correctly. Remember that at STP, the volume of 1 mol of any gas is 22.4 L.

$$6.85\ L\ Br_2 \times \frac{1\ mol\ Br_2}{22.4\ L\ Br_2} \times \frac{2\ mol\ NBr_3}{3\ mol\ Br_2}$$
$$\times \frac{22.4\ L\ NBr_3}{1\ mol\ NBr_3} = 4.57\ L\ NBr_3$$

❸ **Evaluate** **Does the result make sense?**

The mole ratio of NBr_3 to Br_2 in the balanced equation is 2:3. So it makes sense that the volume ratio of NBr_3 to Br_2 (4.57 L:6.85 L) is 2:3 also.

....

2. Carbon monoxide (CO) reacts with hydrogen gas to produce methanol (CH_3OH). How many liters of hydrogen gas will react with 2.5 L of carbon monoxide? Assume conditions are at STP.

$$CO(g) + 2H_2(g) \longrightarrow CH_3OH(l)$$

❶ Analyze List the knowns and the unknown.

Knowns	Unknown
volume of carbon monoxide = 2.5 L CO	volume of hydrogen = ? L H₂
mole ratio = /1 mol CO	
liters CO per mol CO = /1 mol CO	
liters H₂ per mol H₂ = /	

❷ Calculate Solve for the unknown.

Identify the steps needed to convert liters of
CO to liters of H₂.

L CO ⟶ _____ ⟶ _____ ⟶ L H₂

Start with the known volume of CO. Use conversion
factors to calculate the volume of H₂.

$2.5 \text{ L CO} \times \underline{\hspace{2cm}} \times \underline{\hspace{2cm}}$

$\times \underline{\hspace{2cm}} = \underline{\hspace{1cm}} \text{ L H}_2$

❸ Evaluate Does the result make sense?

Is the volume ratio of CO to H₂ the same as the mole ratio? Explain.

_____

_____

On Your Own

3. An average person exhales 450 L of CO₂ a day. How many liters of O₂ can a plant
produce by reacting this amount of CO₂ with excess H₂O? Assume conditions are at STP.

$$6CO_2(g) + 6H_2O(g) \longrightarrow C_6H_{12}O_6(s) + 6O_2(g)$$

4. Boron trifluoride (BF₃) is used to detect radiation levels in the atmosphere. It is
produced by the reaction of boron nitride (BN) with excess fluorine (F₂). Nitrogen gas is
the other product of the reaction. How much nitrogen gas is released if 3.18 L of fluorine
gas reacts? Assume conditions are at STP.

$$2BN(s) + 3F_2(g) \longrightarrow 2BF_3(s) + N_2(g)$$

More Practice Determining a Limiting Reagent

Lesson 12.3

Step-by-Step Practice

1. What is the limiting reagent when 78.0 g $Pb(NO_3)_2$ reacts with 32.5 g NaI? The balanced equation for the reaction of lead nitrate with sodium iodide is:

$$Pb(NO_3)_2(aq) + 2NaI(aq) \longrightarrow PbI_2(s) + 2NaNO_3(aq)$$

❶ Analyze List the knowns and the unknown.

Knowns	Unknown
mass of lead nitrate = 78.0 g $Pb(NO_3)_2$	limiting reagent = ?
mass of sodium iodide = 32.5 g NaI	
1 mol $Pb(NO_3)_2$ = 331.2 g $Pb(NO_3)_2$ (molar mass)	
1 mol NaI = 149.9 g NaI (molar mass)	

❷ Calculate Solve for the unknown.

Find the number of moles of each reactant by converting from mass, in grams, to moles using the molar mass.

$$78.0 \text{ g Pb(NO}_3)_2 \times \frac{1 \text{ mol Pb(NO}_3)_2}{331.2 \text{ g Pb(NO}_3)_2}$$
$$= 0.236 \text{ mol Pb(NO}_3)_2$$

$$32.5 \text{ g NaI} \times \frac{1 \text{ mol NaI}}{149.9 \text{ g NaI}} = 0.217 \text{ mol NaI}$$

Use the coefficients of NaI and $Pb(NO_3)_2$ in the balanced equation to find the mole ratio of NaI to $Pb(NO_3)_2$.

$$\frac{2 \text{ mol NaI}}{1 \text{ mol Pb(NO}_3)_2}$$

Use the mole ratio to find the number of moles of NaI needed to react with 0.236 moles of $Pb(NO_3)_2$.

$$0.236 \text{ mol Pb(NO}_3)_2 \times \frac{2 \text{ mol NaI}}{1 \text{ mol Pb(NO}_3)_2}$$
$$= 0.472 \text{ mol NaI}$$

Compare the actual amount of NaI (0.217 mol) with the amount needed (0.472 mol). The amount needed is greater than the amount available.

The amount of sodium iodide limits the reaction because there is not enough of it to react with all the lead nitrate.

Sodium iodide is the limiting reagent.

❸ Evaluate Does the result make sense?

The ratio of the actual number of moles of NaI to moles of $Pb(NO_3)_2$ is about 1:1, but the mole ratio from the balanced equation is 2:1. So sodium iodide is the limiting reagent.

2. What is the limiting reagent when 277.0 g V_2O_5 reacts with 628.0 g Ca? The balanced equation for the reaction of vanadium peroxide with calcium is:

$$V_2O_5(s) + 5Ca(s) \longrightarrow 5CaO(s) + 2V(s)$$

❶ Analyze List the knowns and the unknown.

Knowns	Unknown
mass of vanadium peroxide = _____ g V_2O_5	limiting reagent = ?
mass of calcium = _____ g Ca	

❷ Calculate Solve for the unknown.

Use the mole ratio to compare the available amounts to what is needed.

$$\text{_____ g } V_2O_5 \times \frac{1 \text{ mol } V_2O_5}{\text{_____}} = \text{_____ mol } V_2O_5$$

$$\text{_____ g Ca} \times \frac{1 \text{ mol Ca}}{\text{_____}} = \text{_____ mol Ca}$$

Convert from mass, in grams, to moles after calculating the molar mass of each reactant.

Find the mole ratio and use it to find the number of moles of Ca needed to react with the actual number of moles of V_2O_5.

$$\text{_____ mol } V_2O_5 \times \frac{\text{_____}}{\text{_____}} = \text{_____ mol Ca}$$

How much Ca is available in the reaction? _____

How much Ca is needed for the reaction? _____

What is the limiting reagent? _____

❸ Evaluate Does the result make sense?

What is the mole ratio of V_2O_5 to Ca from the balanced equation? _____

What is the mole ratio for the actual amounts of V_2O_5 to Ca? _____

On Your Own

3. What is the limiting reagent when 5.81 g CaO reacts with 2.88 g CO_2? The balanced equation for the reaction is:

$$CaO(s) + CO_2(g) \longrightarrow CaCO_3(s)$$

More Practice Calculating Percent Yield

Lesson 12.3

Step-by-Step Practice

1. When 10.0 g of hydrofluoric acid reacts with excess silicon dioxide, silicon fluoride is produced.

$$4HF(g) + SiO_2(s) \longrightarrow SiF_4(g) + 2H_2O(l)$$

What is the theoretical yield of silicon fluoride?

❶ **Analyze** List the knowns and unknowns.

Knowns	Unknown
mass of HF = 10.0 g	theoretical yield = ? g SiF$_4$

❷ **Calculate** Solve for the unknown.

Find the number of moles of the reactant using the molar mass, and then use a mole ratio to calculate the theoretical yield of the product.

molar mass of HF = molar mass of H + molar mass of F

$$= 1.0 \frac{g}{mol} + 19.0 \frac{g}{mol} = 20.0 \frac{g}{mol}$$

molar mass of SiF$_4$ = molar mass of Si + 4 × molar mass of F

Use the periodic table to determine the molar masses of HF and SiF$_4$.

$$= 28.1 \frac{g}{mol} + 4 \times 19.0 \frac{g}{mol} = 104.1 \frac{g}{mol}$$

Use the coefficients of HF and SiF$_4$ in the balanced equation to find the mole ratio.

$$\frac{1 \text{ mol SiF}_4}{4 \text{ mol HF}}$$

Use the molar masses and the mole ratio to find the amount of SiF$_4$ that can form. The theoretical yield is 13.0 g SiF$_4$.

$$10.0 \text{ g HF} \times \frac{1 \text{ mol HF}}{20.0 \text{ g HF}} \times \frac{1 \text{ mol SiF}_4}{4 \text{ mol HF}} \times \frac{104.1 \text{ g SiF}_4}{1 \text{ mol SiF}_4}$$

$$= 13.0 \text{ g SiF}_4$$

❸ **Evaluate** Does the result make sense?

The ratio of the molar masses is about 5:1. This means that there would be 5 times more mass of SiF$_4$ produced as there was of HF if they had a 1:1 mole ratio in the reaction. The mole ratio is actually 1:4, so there are actually $\frac{1}{4}$ as many SiF$_4$ moles in the reaction. With 5 times the mass and $\frac{1}{4}$ of the moles, there is a $\frac{5}{4}$ relationship, slightly larger than 1. So the theoretical mass of SiF$_4$ should be somewhat greater than the given mass of HF, which it is.

2. When 10.0 g of hydrofluoric acid reacts with excess silicon dioxide, 12.0 g of silicon fluoride is produced. The theoretical yield of silicon fluoride is 13.0 g.

$$4HF(g) + SiO_2(s) \longrightarrow SiF_4(g) + 2H_2O(l)$$

What is the percent yield of silicon fluoride?

❶ Analyze List the knowns and unknowns.

Knowns	Unknown
mass of hydrofluoric acid = 10.0 g HF	percent yield = ? %
actual yield of silicon fluoride = 12.0 g SiF_4	
theoretical yield of silicon fluoride = 13.0 g SiF_4	

❷ Calculate Solve for the unknown.

Calculate the percent yield using the ratio of the actual yield and the theoretical yield.

$$\frac{actual\ yield}{theoretical\ yield} \times 100\%$$

The actual amount of silicon fluoride produced is less than the amount that could be produced in a perfect reaction. The percent yield is a way to compare how close the actual yield is to the theoretical yield.

$$\frac{12.0\ g\ SiF_4}{13.0\ g\ SiF_4} \times 100\% = 92.3\%$$

The percent yield is 92.3%.

❸ Evaluate Does the result make sense?

The actual yield is slightly less than the theoretical yield, so a percent yield of 92.3% makes sense.

3. When 9.0 g of potassium hydroxide reacts with excess phosphoric acid, 8.04 g of tripotassium phosphate is produced.

$$3KOH(aq) + H_3PO_4(aq) \longrightarrow K_3PO_4(aq) + 3H_2O(l)$$

What are the theoretical yield and percent yield of tripotassium phosphate?

❶ Analyze List the knowns and unknowns.

Knowns	Unknowns
mass of potassium hydroxide = _____ g KOH	theoretical yield = ? g K_3PO_4
actual yield of tripotassium phosphate = _____ g K_3PO_4	percent yield = ? %
mole ratio = _____/3 mol KOH	

❷ Calculate Solve for the unknown.

Use the periodic table to determine the molar masses of KOH and K_3PO_4.

molar mass of KOH = _____ g/mol

molar mass of K_3PO_4 = _____ g/mol

First, use the molar masses and the mole ratio to convert from the given mass of KOH to the theoretical yield of K_3PO_4.

$$9.0 \text{ g KOH} \times \frac{1 \text{ mol KOH}}{\underline{\hspace{1cm}}} \times \frac{1}{3 \text{ mol KOH}} \times \frac{1}{1 \text{ mol } K_3PO_4}$$

$$= \underline{\hspace{1cm}} \text{ g } K_3PO_4$$

The theoretical yield is = _____ g K_3PO_4.

Then, find the percent yield by taking the ratio of the actual yield and the theoretical yield.

$$\frac{\underline{\hspace{2cm}}}{\underline{\hspace{2cm}}} \times 100\% = \underline{\hspace{1cm}} \%$$

The percent yield is _____%.

❸ Evaluate Does the result make sense?

What is the approximate molar mass ratio of K_3PO_4 to KOH? _____

What is the mole ratio of K_3PO_4 to KOH? _____

Based on these ratios, would you expect the theoretical yield of K_3PO_4 to be greater or less than the mass of KOH? _____

What is the actual mass of K_3PO_4? _____

What is the theoretical yield of K_3PO_4? _____

Based on these masses, would you expect the percent yield to be close to 100% or much less than 100%? _____

On Your Own

4. Magnesium nitrate is a chemical in plant fertilizer. It is produced by the reaction of magnesium and excess silver nitrate.

$$Mg(s) + 2AgNO_3(aq) \longrightarrow 2Mg(NO_3)_2(aq) + 2Ag(s)$$

What is the theoretical yield of silver if a 5.5 g strip of magnesium reacts? What is the percent yield of silver if 40.0 g is produced in the reaction?

5. Lithium nitrate, $LiNO_3$, is a chemical used to create red fireworks. It is produced by the reaction of lithium nitride, Li_3N, and excess ammonium nitrate, NH_4NO_3.

$$Li_3N(aq) + 3NH_4NO_3(aq) \longrightarrow 3LiNO_3(aq) + (NH_4)_3N(aq)$$

What is the percent yield of $LiNO_3$ if 30.0 g is actually produced when 6.0 g of Li_3N reacts? *Hint:* Calculate the theoretical yield of $LiNO_3$ before finding the percent yield.

6. The reaction of selenium hexachloride, $SeCl_6$, with excess oxygen produces selenium dioxide, SeO_2, and chlorine gas.

$$SeCl_6(s) + O_2(g) \longrightarrow SeO_2(s) + 3Cl_2(g)$$

What are the theoretical yields of SeO_2 and Cl_2 if 9.0 g of $SeCl_6$ reacts? What are the percent yields if 3.0 g SeO_2 and 6.5 g Cl_2 are actually produced? *Hint:* Calculate the yields of each product separately.

12 Standardized Test Prep Tutor

Read the question. The highlighted words tell you what you need to find.

Notes and Calculations

1. Nitric acid is formed by the reaction of nitrogen dioxide with water.

   $$3NO_2(g) + H_2O(l) \longrightarrow NO(g) + 2HNO_3(aq)$$

   How many moles of water are needed to react with 8.4 mol NO_2?

   (A) 2.8 mol   **(C)** 8.4 mol
   (B) 3.0 mol   **(D)** 25 mol

   ❶ Analyze

   Use the mole ratio from the balanced equation to find the amount of water needed for the reaction.

   ❷ Solve

   Use the coefficients of H_2O and NO_2 in the balanced equation to find the mole ratio. Place mol NO_2 in the denominator so this factor will cancel in the calculation.

   Multiply the known quantity of NO_2 by the mole ratio. Remember to cancel units in the calculations.

   ❸ Choose an Answer

   Find the answer that matches your calculation.

   $$\frac{1 \text{ mol } H_2O}{3 \text{ mol } NO_2}$$

   $$8.4 \text{ mol } NO_2 \times \frac{1 \text{ mol } H_2O}{3 \text{ mol } NO_2}$$
   $$= 2.8 \text{ mol } H_2O$$

   The correct answer is A.

   Now you try it.

   The combustion of propane produces carbon dioxide and water vapor.

   $$C_3H_8(g) + 5O_2(g) \longrightarrow 3CO_2(g) + 4H_2O(g)$$

   The reaction produces 3.2 moles of water. How many moles of carbon dioxide are produced?

   (A) 4.3 mol   **(C)** 2.4 mol
   (B) 4.0 mol   **(D)** 0.8 mol

   Barium oxide and aluminum can react to produce aluminum oxide and barium.

   $$3BaO(s) + 2Al(s) \longrightarrow Al_2O_3(s) + 3Ba(s)$$

   How many moles of BaO can produce 1.5 mol Al_2O_3?

   (A) 2.0 mol   **(C)** 0.5 mol
   (B) 4.5 mol   **(D)** 0.8 mol

Use the reaction below to answer Questions 4 and 5.

T_2 Q_2 T_3Q

4. Write a balanced equation for the reaction between element T and element Q.

   Write the skeleton equation.

   Make a table showing the elements involved in the reaction. Count the number of atoms of each element on both sides of the equation.

   The equation is not balanced because there are more Q atoms as reactants than products.

   Add a coefficient of 2 to the product to balance Q.

   The number of Qs on each side of the equation is now balanced. Now there are more T atoms as products than reactants.

   Add a coefficient of 3 in front of the T_2 reactants.

   Check to make sure there are the same number of reactant atoms and product atoms for each element.

   The equation is balanced.

$T_2 + Q_2 \longrightarrow T_3Q$

Element	Reactant	Product
T	2	3
Q	2	1

$T_2 + Q_2 \longrightarrow 2T_3Q$

Element	Reactant	Product
T	2	$3 \times 2 = 6$
Q	2	$1 \times 2 = 2$

$3T_2 + Q_2 \longrightarrow 2T_3Q$

Element	Reactant	Product
T	$2 \times 3 = 6$	6
Q	2	2

5. Based on the atomic windows, identify the limiting reagent.

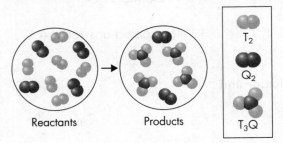

Reactants   Products T_2 Q_2 T_3Q

Look at the atomic window for the products. Some molecules of Q_2 are left over, but no molecules of T_2 remain. The amount of T_2 limited the amount of product that could form.

Now you try it.

Use the reaction and the atomic windows to answer the following two questions.

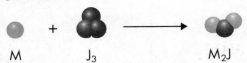

M J_3 M_2J

Write a balanced equation for the reaction between element M and element J.

Identify the limiting reagent.

The limiting reagent is T_2.

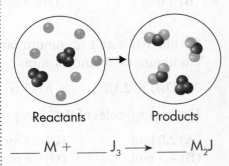

Reactants   Products

____ M + ____ $J_3 \longrightarrow$ ____ M_2J

The limiting reagent is ____.

Interpret Graphs

Distribution of Molecular Kinetic Energy

Lesson 13.1

Preview the Graph

The graph shows the distribution of kinetic energy of water at two different temperatures. The molecules in each sample of water have a wide range of kinetic energies.

Look at the key on the right side of the graph. The black curve represents the distribution of energy in hot water.

What does the blue curve represent?

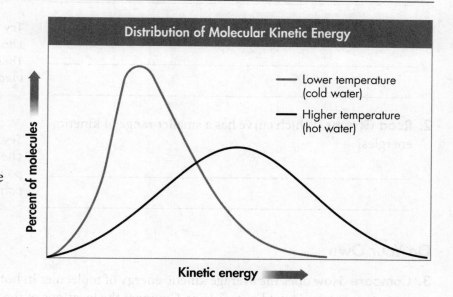

_____

_____

Look at the *x*-axis. The variable is kinetic energy. What does the arrow pointing to the right show?

_____

_____

The *y*-axis shows the percent of molecules with the same kinetic energy. The percentage of molecules increases from bottom to top along the axis.

Analyze the Graph

Now you are ready to answer some more questions. As you read the questions:

▶ Highlight key words.

▶ Circle numbers and units.

Use the first question as an example.

1. **Read Graphs** Describe and compare the shape of each curve.

_____

_____

_____

> Try it! Use your finger to trace the blue curve from left to right. Then use your finger to trace the black curve.

2. **Read Graphs** Which curve has a smaller range of kinetic energies?

_____

_____

> Try it! Both curves begin at the same point. Look for the point where both curves end and compare the width of each.

On Your Own

3. **Compare** How does the average kinetic energy of molecules in hot water compare to that of molecules in cold water? *Hint:* Compare the locations of the peaks.

_____

_____

4. **Predict** What would happen to the shape of the curve if the water were room temperature? *Hint:* Room temperature is between the temperatures for hot water and cold water.

_____

_____

_____

5. **Predict** What would happen to the shape of the curve if the water temperature were even lower than the cold water sample?

_____

_____

6. **Draw Conclusions** When the temperature of a substance decreases, what happens to the average kinetic energy of the substance?

_____

Interpret Data Comparing Vapor Pressures

Lesson 13.2

Preview the Table

Vapor Pressure (in kPa) of Three Substances at Different Temperatures						
Substance	0°C	20°C	40°C	60°C	80°C	100°C
Water	0.61	2.33	7.37	19.92	47.34	101.33
Ethanol	1.63	5.85	18.04	47.02	108.34	225.75
Diethyl ether	24.70	58.96	122.80	230.65	399.11	647.87

The table shows the vapor pressures of some liquids at different temperatures. Vapor pressure is a measure of the force exerted by a gas above a liquid.

What are the units of vapor pressure in the table?

_____

_____

Look at the first column, labeled Substance. What three liquids are being compared in the table?

_____

_____

Vapor pressure data are given for six different temperatures, from 0°C to 100°C. By what interval does the temperature increase as you move across a row from left to right?

_____

_____

Recall that the higher the temperature of a liquid, the more energy the particles have and the more likely they are to evaporate.

Analyze the Table

Now you are ready to answer some more questions. As you read the questions:

▶ Highlight key words.

▶ Circle numbers and units.

Use the first question as an example.

1. Read Tables What is the vapor pressure of water at 20°C?

_____

_____

> Try it! Find the row for water. Move across the row until you reach the 20°C column. Give your answer in kPa.

2. **Describe** How does the vapor pressure of water change from left to right across the table?

_____

_____

> **Try it!** Find the row for water. Move across the row from left to right, and look to see if the values for the vapor pressure increase or decrease.

3. **Compare** How do the vapor pressures of the three liquids compare at 20°C?

_____

_____

> **Try it!** Find the 20°C column. Look at the vapor pressure values for each liquid. Describe how the values of the vapor pressures compare: are they about the same or is one larger than another?

On Your Own

5. **Compare** Describe the pattern shown in the table for the vapor pressure of the three substances between 0°C and 100°C.

_____

6. **Draw Conclusions** How does an increase in temperature affect the ability of molecules to evaporate from a liquid?

_____

_____

7. **Infer** For every temperature in the table, diethyl ether has a higher vapor pressure than water or ethanol. What does that say about the relative strength of attraction between the particles of each liquid?

_____

_____

Interpret Graphs Vapor Pressure vs. Temperature Lesson 13.2

Preview the Graph

Read the title of the graph. This graph shows the relationship between the vapor pressure and temperature. Vapor pressure is a measure of the force exerted by a gas above a liquid. The four labeled curves show the vapor pressures of different liquids.

The dark blue curve shows the vapor pressure of chloroform. What substances do the rest of the vapor pressure curves show?

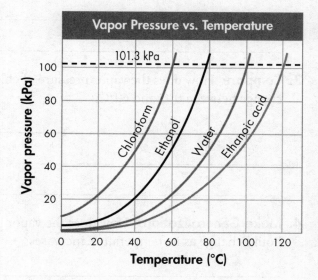

_____

_____

Vapor pressure is the variable on the *y*-axis.
Temperature in degrees Celsius (°C) is the variable on the *x*-axis.

What happens to the temperature as you move from left to right across the graph?

_____

The dashed line at the top of the graph is the line for standard air pressure (101.3 kPa). Find the points where the vapor pressure curves cross the dashed line. These points mark the boiling point of each liquid at standard pressure.

Analyze the Graph

Now you are ready to answer some more questions. As you read the questions:

► Highlight key words.
► Circle numbers and units.

Use the first question as an example.

1. Read Graphs Estimate the boiling point of water at standard pressure.

_____

> **Try it!** Find the point where the water curve crosses the dashed line. Trace the vertical line down to the x-axis.

2. Read Graphs At standard pressure, which substance is a gas at 70°C?

_____

_____

> **Try it!** Draw a line up from 70°C on the x-axis to the dashed line. Find the curve that crosses the dashed line at a point to the left of your vertical line.

3. Compare How does the vapor pressure of chloroform change between 0°C and 60°C?

_____

_____

_____

> **Try it!** Find the curve for chloroform at 0°C on the x-axis. Estimate the value on the y-axis for that point. Repeat for 60°C on the x-axis.

4. Make Generalizations How does the vapor pressure of a liquid change as its temperature increases?

_____

_____

> **Try it!** As you move from left to right across the x-axis, look to see if the vapor pressure values of the curves increase or decrease.

On Your Own

5. Read Graphs Estimate the boiling point of ethanol at standard pressure.

_____

6. Read Graphs At standard pressure, which substances are liquids at 90°C?

_____

7. Predict What air pressure would be needed for water to boil at 80°C?

_____

_____

Interpret Graphs Phase Diagram of Water Lesson 13.4

Preview the Graph

A phase diagram shows how temperature and pressure affect the three phases of water.

Pressure, in kPa, is the unit on the y-axis. What is the unit on the x-axis?

_____

The solid black lines on the diagram separate the different phase regions. At any point along one of these lines, the two phases are in equilibrium and phase changes can occur.

Dashed horizontal and vertical lines connect each of the labeled points to the y-axis and the x-axis.

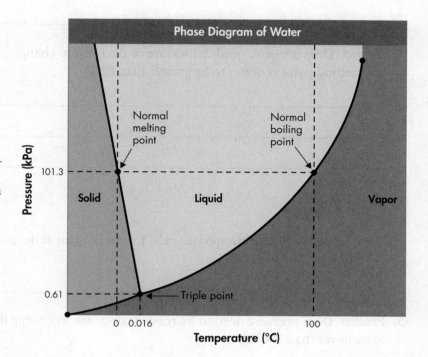

The normal melting and boiling points mark where those phase changes normally occur with standard atmospheric pressure.

Find the point for the normal melting point of water. The pressure at the point is normal atmospheric pressure (101.3 kPa). What is the temperature at that point?

_____

_____

Analyze the Graph

Now you are ready to answer some more questions. As you read the questions:

► Highlight key words.
► Circle numbers and units.

Use the first question as an example.

1. Read Graphs Find the triple point. This is the point where all three phases exist in equilibrium. What are the values of the temperature and pressure at the triple point?

_____

_____

> **Try it!** Place your finger on the triple point. Use the dashed lines to find the values on the x-axis and the y-axis.

2. Read Graphs Which two phases exist in equilibrium at the
normal boiling point of water?

_____

_____

Try it! Find the normal boiling
point and look for the phases
on either side of the solid
black line.

3. Predict Does pressure need to increase or decrease to change
the melting point of water to be greater than 0°C?

_____

_____

_____

Try it! Find the normal
melting point of water. Follow
the black line down towards
increased temperature. Did
the pressure increase or
decrease?

On Your Own

4. Read Graphs Which two phases exist in equilibrium at the normal melting point
of water?

_____

5. Predict Does pressure need to increase or decrease to change the boiling point of water
to be lower than 100°C?

_____

_____

6. Read Graphs Find the normal boiling point of water. What would the phase be if the
pressure were decreased but the temperature remained the same?

_____

7. Read Graphs At standard pressure (101.3 kPa), is there any temperature where water
exists as a solid, liquid and gas at the same time? Explain your answer.

_____

_____

13 Standardized Test Prep Tutor

Use this graph to answer Questions 1 and 2.

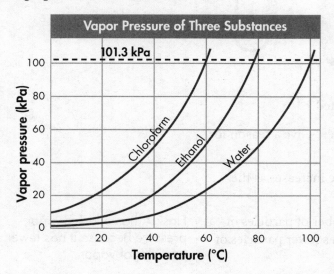

Vapor Pressure of Three Substances

The highlighted words tell you which curve on the graph to use to answer each question.

1. What is the normal boiling point of ethanol?

The normal boiling point of ethanol is the temperature at which it boils at standard pressure (101.3 kPa).

Look at the curve for ethanol. Where does it cross the 101.3 kPa line? It crosses just before the vertical line for 80°C. So the boiling point will be a bit less than 80°C.

The normal boiling point of ethanol ≈ 78°C.

2. Can chloroform be heated to 90°C in an open container?

Recall that the temperature of a liquid stops rising when the liquid begins to boil. So the question is really asking whether 90°C is higher or lower than chloroform's normal boiling point.

Look at the curve for chloroform. It crosses the 101.3 kPa line at a temperature of about 60°C. This is the boiling point of chloroform at standard pressure.

Chloroform cannot be heated to 90°C in an open container.

Now you try it.

Can ethanol be heated to 70°C in an open container?
Explain your answer.

_____

_____

Can ethanol be heated to 80°C in an open container?
Explain your answer.

_____

_____

Use this drawing to answer Questions 4–5. The same liquid is in each flask.

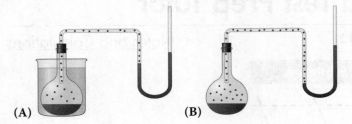

(A)   (B)

In each question, the key phrase is highlighted.

4. In which flask is the vapor pressure lower? Give a reason for your answer.

   In a closed container, the vapor pressure increases as the number of particles of vapor increases.

   Look at the drawing. Compare the number of particles of vapor in Flask A and Flask B. Flask A has fewer particles of vapor.

   Flask A has a lower vapor pressure because it has fewer particles of vapor.

5. In which flask is the liquid at the higher temperature? Explain your answer.

   An increase in temperature causes an increase in average kinetic energy. More particles have enough energy to escape from the liquid, and the vapor pressure increases.

   Look at the drawing again. The flask that has more particles of vapor will be at the higher temperature.

   Flask B is at the higher temperature.

Now you try it.

The liquid in Flask C is the same as the liquid in Flask A. But the temperature in Flask C is lower than the temperature in Flask A. Use the drawing to model the vapor pressure at the lower temperature. Add particles of vapor and draw the level of mercury you would expect. *Hint:* Use the differences between the drawings of Flask A and Flask B to help you determine the correct level of mercury.

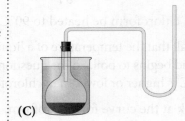

(C)

Interpret Graphs Boyle's Law

Lesson 14.2

Preview the Graph

Study the line graph. Volume in liters (L) is on the x-axis. Pressure in kilopascals (kPa) is on the y-axis. This graph shows the relationship between the pressure and volume of a gas as described by Boyle. The drawings can help you picture the volume of the gas at specific points.

Find and circle Point A. Describe the drawing. Record the number of particles.

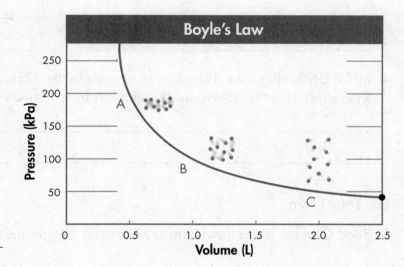

_____

_____

_____

_____

Find and circle Point B. Look at the drawing. What happened to the volume in the cylinder? What happened to the amount of gas?

_____

_____

Analyze the Graph

Now you are ready to answer some more questions. As you read the questions:

▶ Highlight key words.

▶ Circle numbers and units.

Use the first question as an example.

1. Read Graphs When the volume is ⓪.5 L, what is the pressure?

_____

> **Try it!** Find 0.5 on the x-axis. Follow the vertical line to Point A. Follow the horizontal line to the value for pressure.

2. Read Graphs At Point B, what are the values for volume and pressure?

_____

> **Try it!** Find Point B. Follow the lines from the point to the x-axis and the y-axis.

3. Compare How did the volume of the gas change between Points A and B? How did the pressure change?

_____

_____

_____

> **Try it!** Compare the values for volume at Points A and B. Then compare the values for pressure at Points A and B. Use increased and decreased in your answer.

4. Make Generalizations How does an increase in the volume of a gas affect its pressure? Assume the temperature is constant.

_____

_____

> **Try it!** Begin your answer with "When the volume of a gas increases ..."

On Your Own

5. Read Graphs When the volume is 2 L, what is the pressure?

_____

6. Predict Use the pressure at 2.0 L to predict the pressure at 4.0 L. Explain your answer.

_____

_____

7. Estimate What would the pressure be if the volume were 1.5 L? *Hint:* Draw a line between the point for 1.5 L and the y-axis.

_____

8. Classify Is the relationship between the pressure and volume of a gas a direct one or an inverse one? *Hint:* Choose *direct* if both variables increase or decrease at the same time. Choose *inverse* if one variable increases while the other decreases.

_____

_____

More Practice Using Boyle's Law

Step-by-Step Practice

1. A gas with a volume of 2.2 L at 140 kPa expands to fill a 4.4-L container. What is the pressure in the new container? The temperature does not change.

❶ **Analyze** List the knowns and the unknown.

Knowns	Unknown
$P_1 = 140$ kPa	$P_2 = ?$
$V_1 = 2.2$ L	
$V_2 = 4.4$ L	

❷ **Calculate** Solve for the unknown.

Divide both sides of Boyle's law by V_2 to isolate the unknown. Rewrite the equation so the unknown is on the left.

$$\frac{P_1 \times V_1}{V_2} = \frac{P_2 \times \cancel{V_2}}{\cancel{V_2}}$$

$$P_2 = \frac{P_1 \times V_1}{V_2}$$

Substitute the knowns into the equation and solve.

$$P_2 = \frac{140 \text{ kPa} \times 2.2\,\cancel{L}}{4.4\,\cancel{L}} = \frac{308 \text{ kPa}}{4.4} = 70 \text{ kPa}$$

❸ **Evaluate** Does the result make sense?

The answer agrees with Boyle's law. As the volume increased from 2.2 L to 4.4 L, the pressure decreased from 140 kPa to 70 kPa.

....

2. The pressure on a 5.67 L sample of gas decreases from 321 kPa to 115 kPa. What is the new volume?

❶ **Analyze** List the knowns and the unknown.

❷ **Calculate** Solve for the unknown.

Knowns	Unknown
$V_1 = $ _____	$V_2 = ?$
$P_1 = $ _____	
$P_2 = $ _____	

Rearrange Boyle's law to isolate the unknown. $V_2 =$ _____

Substitute the knowns into the equation and solve. $V_2 =$ _____ =

❸ Evaluate Does the result make sense?

_____

_____

_____

On Your Own

3. A sample of gas has a volume of 5.00 L at 225 kPa. If the volume is reduced to 2.50 L, what will the pressure be?

4. A sample of gas in a 1.40 L container at 475 kPa expands to fill a 3.50 L container. What is the new gas pressure?

5. When a piston is pushed down in a cylinder, the pressure on the gas in the cylinder increases from 125 kPa to 375 kPa. The initial volume is 3.3 L. What is the final volume?

Interpret Graphs Charles's Law

Lesson 14.2

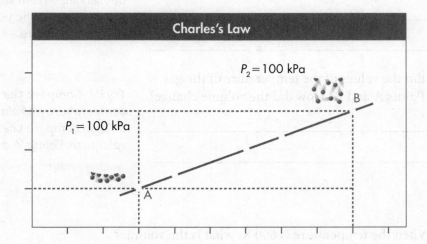

Preview the Graph

Study the line graph. This graph shows the relationship between the volume and the temperature of a gas at constant pressure.

Volume is the variable on the y-axis. What units are used for the volume?

_____

What is the variable on the x-axis? What are the units?

_____

The drawings can help you picture the volume of the gas at two specific points. The amount of gas and the pressure of the gas are constant. Only the temperature and the volume are changing. The symbol Δ means "a change in". What do ΔT and ΔV stand for?

_____

Analyze the Graph

Now you are ready to answer some more questions. As you read the questions:

▶ Highlight key words.
▶ Circle numbers and units.

Use the first question as an example.

1. **Read Graphs** What is the volume of the gas when the temperature is 300 K?

_____

> **Try it!** Find 300 K on the x-axis. Trace up from the axis to Point A. Follow the horizontal line to the value for volume.

2. Read Graphs At Point B, what are the values for
temperature and volume?

_____

_____

> **Try it!** Find Point B. Follow the dotted lines from the point to the x-axis and the y-axis and record the values.

3. Compare How did the values of the temperature of the gas
change between Points A and B? How did the volume change?

_____

_____

> **Try it!** Compare the values for temperature at Points A and B. Then compare the values for volume at Points A and B.

On Your Own

4. Read Graphs When the temperature is 600 K, what is the volume?

_____

5. Predict If the temperature of a gas were 0 K, what would the volume of the gas be?

_____

6. Predict Use the volume at 600 K to predict the volume at 1200 K. Explain your answer.
Hint: How did the volume change when the temperature went from 300 K to 600 K?

_____

_____

7. Make Generalizations How does an increase in the temperature of a gas affect its
volume? Assume the pressure is constant.

_____

_____

8. Classify Based on the shape of the graph, is the relationship between the volume and
temperature of a gas a direct relationship or an inverse relationship? *Hint:* Choose *direct*
if both variables increase or decrease at the same time. Choose *inverse* if one variable
increases while the other decreases.

_____

_____

More Practice Using Charles's Law

Step-by-Step Practice

1. An inflated balloon has a volume of 3.85 L at 24°C. The balloon is placed in a refrigerator and cooled to 4.0°C. What is the new volume of the balloon? Assume the pressure does not change.

❶ Analyze List the knowns and the unknown.

Knowns	Unknown
$V_1 = 3.85$ L	$V_2 = ?$
$T_1 = 24°C$	
$T_2 = 4°C$	

❷ Calculate Solve for the unknown.

When you use Charles's law, the temperatures must be in kelvins. To convert temperature in °C to kelvins, add 273.

$$T_1 = 24°C + 273 = 297 \text{ K}$$
$$T_2 = 4°C + 273 = 277 \text{ K}$$

Multiply Charles's law by T_2 to isolate the unknown, V_2.

$$T_2 \times \frac{V_1}{T_1} = \frac{V_2}{T_2} \times T_2$$

$$\frac{V_1 \times T_2}{T_1} = V_2$$

Then rearrange the equation so the unknown is on the left.

$$V_2 = \frac{V_1 \times T_2}{T_1}$$

Substitute the knowns into the equation, and solve.

$$V_2 = \frac{3.85 \text{ L} \times 277 \text{ K}}{297 \text{ K}} = 3.59 \text{ L}$$

❸ Evaluate Does the result make sense?

The answer agrees with Charles's law. As the temperature decreased, the volume decreased.

2. A sample of neon gas has a volume of 22.8 L when the temperature is 28°C. What is the volume of the same gas at 15°C? Assume the pressure does not change.

❶ Analyze List the knowns and the unknown.

Knowns	Unknown
$V_1 = $ _____	$V_2 = ?$
$T_1 = $ _____	
$T_2 = $ _____	

❷ Calculate Solve for the unknown.

Change the temperatures from °C to kelvins.

$T_1 = $ _____ °C + 273 = _____ K

$T_2 = $ _____ °C + 273 = _____ K

Rearrange the Charles's law equation so the unknown is on the left.

$V_2 = $

Substitute the knowns into the equation, and solve.

$V_2 = $

❸ Evaluate Does the result make sense?

_____

_____

On Your Own

3. At 31°C, the volume of gas in a small plastic bag is 0.115 L. If you place the bag in a cooler at 12°C, what is the new volume? Assume the pressure is constant.

4. A 6.70-L sample of argon gas is in a cylinder with a piston. The temperature is 242 K. If the pressure is kept constant, at what temperature will the volume of the gas be 7.30 L?

5. Nitrogen gas is transferred from a 12.1 L container to a 15.2 L container at constant pressure. The temperature of the gas in the second container is 35.4°C. What was the temperature in the first container?

More Practice Using the Combined Gas Law   Lesson 14.2

Step-by-Step Practice

1. A beach ball is partly inflated to a volume of 23.3 L.
The temperature of the air in the ball is 305 K,
and its pressure is 101.3 kPa. A swimmer holds
the ball under water in a pool, where the pressure is
131.3 kPa. The volume of air in the ball decreases to
17.6 L. What happens to the temperature
of the air in the ball?

❶ **Analyze** **List the knowns and the unknown.**

Knowns	Unknown
$V_1 = 23.3$ L	$T_2 = ?$ K
$T_1 = 305$ K	
$P_1 = 101.3$ kPa	
$V_2 = 17.6$ L	
$P_2 = 131.3$ kPa	

❷ **Calculate** **Solve for the unknown.**

When you are dealing with volume, temperature, and
pressure, you need to use the combined gas law.

$$\frac{P_1 \times V_1}{T_1} = \frac{P_2 \times V_2}{T_2}$$

Rearrange the equation to isolate the unknown, T_2.
First, multiply both sides of the equation by T_2 so T_2
moves from the denominator to the numerator.

$$T_2 \times \frac{P_1 \times V_1}{T_1} = \frac{P_2 \times V_2}{\cancel{T_2}} \times \cancel{T_2}$$

$$T_2 \times \frac{\cancel{T_1}}{\cancel{P_1 \times V_1}} \times \frac{\cancel{P_1 \times V_1}}{\cancel{T_1}} = \frac{P_2 \times V_2 \times T_1}{P_1 \times V_1}$$

Next, multiply both sides of the equation by T_1
and divide both sides of the equation by $P_1 \times V_1$.

$$T_2 = \frac{P_2 \times V_2 \times T_1}{P_1 \times V_1}$$

Substitute the knowns into the equation, and solve.

$$T_2 = \frac{131.3 \text{ kPa} \times 17.6 \cancel{L} \times 305 \text{ K}}{101.3 \text{ kPa} \times 23.3 \cancel{L}} = 299 \text{ K}$$

❸ **Evaluate** **Does the result make sense?**

A decrease in volume and an increase in pressure have
opposite effects on the temperature. To evaluate the
overall change in temperature, look at the ratios in the
equation. Multiply T_1 by the ratio P_2/P_1 (1.30) and the
ratio V_2/V_1 (0.755). The result is 299 K.

2. Neon gas at 25°C and 101.3 kPa is compressed in a rigid container to a volume of 84.6 L. What is the pressure of this gas at 88.5 L and 28°C?

❶ Analyze List the knowns and the unknown.

Knowns	Unknown
$V_1 = 84.6$ L	$P_2 = ?$ K
$T_1 = 25°C$	
$P_1 = 101.3$ kPa	
$V_2 = $ _____	
$T_2 = $ _____	

❷ Calculate Solve for the unknown.

First, convert temperature in °C to kelvins.

$T_1 = $ _____ C° + 273 = _____ K

$T_2 = $ _____ C° + 273 = _____ K

Rearrange the combined gas law to isolate the unknown, P_2.

T_2 and V_2 are on the same side of the equation as P_2. You need to multiply both sides of the equation by T_2 and divide both sides of the equation by V_2.

$$ \underline{} \times \frac{\times}{\underline{}} = \frac{\times}{\underline{}} \times \underline{} $$

Rewrite the equation so that the unknown is on the left.

$$ P_2 = \frac{\times \quad \times}{\times} $$

Substitute the knowns into the equation, and solve.

$$ P_2 = \frac{\times \quad \times}{\times} $$

$$ = $$

❸ Evaluate Does the result make sense?

Use the ratios for the change in volume and temperature to evaluate the overall change in pressure.

$$ \frac{V_1}{V_2} = \underline{} \qquad \frac{T_1}{T_2} = \underline{} $$

What is the product of the ratios and P_1. _____

Does this value match your answer? _____

On Your Own

3. A gas has a volume of 275 L at 348 K. When it is cooled to 297 K, its pressure changes to 115 kPa and its volume decreases to 263 L. What was the original pressure of the gas?

More Practice Using the Ideal Gas Law

Lesson 14.3

Step-by-Step Practice

1. Argon gas in a storage tank has a volume of 225 L at 643 kPa and 24.6°C. How many moles of argon gas are in the tank?

❶ **Analyze** List the knowns and the unknown.

Knowns	Unknown
$P = 643 \text{ kPa}$	$n = ? \text{ mol Ar}$
$V = 225 \text{ L}$	
$R = 8.31 \text{ L} \cdot \text{kPa/K} \cdot \text{mol}$	
$T = 24.6°C$	

❷ **Calculate** Solve for the unknown.

Before you use the ideal gas law, you must first convert temperature to kelvins.

$$T = 24.6°C + 273 = 297.6 \text{ K}$$

Rearrange the ideal gas law to isolate the unknown. Rewrite the equation so the unknown is on the left.

$$P \times V = n \times R \times T$$
$$n = \frac{P \times V}{R \times T}$$

Substitute the knowns into the equation, and solve. $n = \dfrac{643 \text{ kPa} \times 225 \text{ L}}{8.31 \dfrac{\text{L} \cdot \text{kPa}}{\text{K} \cdot \text{mol}} \times 297.6 \text{ K}} = 58.5 \text{ mol Ar}$

❸ **Evaluate** Does the result make sense?

It is reasonable that a large volume of argon gas at a high pressure would contain a large number of moles.

....

2. A balloon at STP contains 1.19 mol of helium. How many liters of helium are in the balloon?
   Hint: At STP, $P = 101.3 \text{ kPa}$ and $T = 293 \text{ K}$.

❶ **Analyze** List the knowns and the unknown.

Knowns	Unknown
$P = $ _____	$V = ? \text{ L He}$
$n = $ _____	
$R = $ _____	
$T = $ _____	

❷ Calculate **Solve for the unknown.**

Rearrange the ideal gas law to isolate the unknown. Rewrite the equation so the unknown is on the left.

$$P \times V = n \times R \times T$$

$$V = \underline{\hspace{2cm}}$$

Substitute the knowns into the equation and solve. $\quad V = \underline{\hspace{4cm}}$

$$= \underline{\hspace{2cm}}$$

❸ Evaluate **Does the result make sense?**

The volume for 1 mole of gas at STP is around 24 L. How many liters would you expect 1.19 moles to fill?

_____

On Your Own

3. An energy-efficient window consists of a layer of argon gas between two glass plates. There are 0.0388 mol of argon gas in a volume of 0.976 L. What is the pressure of the gas if the temperature is 35.8°C? *Hint:* K = °C + 273

4. A 12.0-L cylinder contains oxygen gas (O_2) at a pressure of 20,000 kPa and a temperature of 298 K. How many moles of gas are in the cylinder?

5. An aerosol canister contains 0.662 mol of gas at a pressure of 100 kPa. If the temperature of the gas is 27°C, what is the volume of gas in the canister?

Interpret Data Composition of Dry Air

Lesson 14.4

Preview the Table

The table compares the volume and pressure of the main components of dry air. Look at the Volume column. The volume of each component is given as a percent. The percentages add up to 100. What are the two main components of dry air?

_____

_____

Composition of Dry Air		
Component	Volume (%)	Partial Pressure (kPa)
Nitrogen	78.08	79.11
Oxygen	20.95	21.23
Carbon dioxide	0.04	0.04
Argon and others	0.93	0.94
Total	100.00	

The third column lists the partial pressure of each component. What units are used for partial pressure?

_____

_____

Analyze the Data

Now you are ready to answer some more questions. As you read the questions:

▶ Highlight key words.
▶ Circle numbers and units.

Use the first question as an example.

1. Read Tables What is the percent by volume of nitrogen in dry air? What is the percent by volume of oxygen?

_____

> Try it! In the second column, find the values for nitrogen and oxygen.

2. Read Tables What is the partial pressure of nitrogen? What is the partial pressure of oxygen?

_____

> Try it! In the third column, find the values for nitrogen and oxygen.

3. Estimate About how many times greater is the percent by volume of nitrogen than the percent by volume of oxygen in dry air?

_____

> Try it! Round up the value for nitrogen and round down the value for oxygen to values that are multiples of 10. Then divide.

On Your Own

4. Read Tables What percent by volume of dry air is carbon dioxide? What is the partial pressure of carbon dioxide?

_____

5. Read Tables What component of dry air has a partial pressure of 0.94 kPa?

_____

6. Calculate Use the values in the table to find the total pressure of dry air.

_____

7. Identify What unit is equal to the value of the answer to Question 6? *Hint:* This unit is used as a standard.

_____

8. Predict At higher altitudes, atmospheric pressure is lower than at sea level. What do you think happens to the partial pressure of each gas as the altitude increases? Explain your answer.

_____

_____

9. Draw Conclusions Air usually contains some water vapor. The amount of water vapor can vary from a trace to about 4 percent. Why do you think water vapor was not included in the data?

_____

_____

More Practice Using Dalton's Law of Partial Pressures   Lesson 14.4

Step-by-Step Practice

1. A mixture of krypton gas (Kr), argon gas (Ar), and xenon gas (Xe) is in a closed container. The total pressure in the container is 326 kPa. If the partial pressure of krypton is 42 kPa and the partial pressure of argon is 208 kPa. What is the partial pressure of xenon gas?

   ❶ Analyze List the knowns and the unknown.

Knowns	Unknown
$P_{total} = 326\,kPa$	$P_{Xe} = ?\,kPa$
$P_{Kr} = 42\,kPa$	
$P_{Ar} = 208\,kPa$	

   ❷ Calculate Solve for the unknown.

   Start with the equation for Dalton's law of partial pressures.

   $$P_{total} = P_{Kr} + P_{Ar} + P_{Xe}$$

   Subtract P_{Kr} and P_{Ar} from both sides of the equation to isolate P_{Xe}.

   $$P_{total} - P_{Kr} - P_{Ar} = P_{Xe}$$

   Rewrite the equation so that the unknown is on the left side.

   $$P_{Xe} = P_{total} - P_{Kr} - P_{Ar}$$

   Substitute the knowns into the equation and solve.

   $$P_{Xe} = 326\,kPa - 42\,kPa - 208\,kPa$$

   $$P_{Xe} = 76\,kPa$$

   ❸ Evaluate Does the result make sense?

   To evaluate your answer, add up the partial pressures: $42 + 208 + 76 = 326\,kPa$. Because the sum of the partial pressures equals the total pressure, the answer makes sense.

   ....

2. Some lasers rely on a mixture of gases. In one gas laser, a mixture of carbon dioxide (CO_2), nitrogen gas (N_2), and hydrogen gas (H_2) has a total pressure of 1.00 atm. If P_{CO_2} is 0.39 atm and P_{N_2} is 0.24 atm, what is the partial pressure of the hydrogen gas?

❶ Analyze List the knowns and the unknown.

Knowns	Unknown
$P_{total} =$ _____	$P_{H_2} = ?\ kPa$
$P_{CO_2} =$ _____	
$P_{N_2} =$ _____	

❷ Calculate Solve for the unknown.

Start with the equation for Dalton's law of partial pressures.

$$P_{total} = P_{CO_2} + P_{N_2} + P_{H_2}$$

Rearrange the equation to isolate P_{H_2}.

$$P_{total} - P_{CO_2} - P_{N_2} = \underline{\quad\quad}$$

Rewrite the equation so that the unknown is on the left side.

$$P_{H_2} = P_{total} - \underline{\quad} - \underline{\quad}$$

Substitute the knowns into the equation and solve for P_{H_2}.

$$P_{H_2} = \underline{\quad}\ atm - \underline{\quad}\ atm - \underline{\quad}\ atm = \underline{\quad\quad}$$

❸ Evaluate Does the result make sense?

The combined pressures of carbon dioxide and nitrogen _____ of the total are about two-thirds of the total pressure. What must the partial pressure of hydrogen be for the result to make sense?

On Your Own

3. To keep food from spoiling, a package of food stored at 1.00 atm is injected with a mixture of argon (Ar), nitrogen (N_2), and sulfur dioxide (SO_2). The partial pressure of argon is 0.49 atm, and the partial pressure of nitrogen is 0.15 atm. What is the partial pressure of sulfur dioxide?

4. A thermos contains a mixture of nitrogen (N_2), hydrogen (H_2), and oxygen (O_2) at a total pressure of 101.3 kPa. The partial pressure of hydrogen is 24.1 kPa, and the partial pressure of oxygen is 4.1 kPa. What is the partial pressure of nitrogen in the thermos?

14 Standardized Test Prep Tutor

Read the question. The term with the blue highlight tells you what you need to solve for. Circle numbers and units.

1. A gas in a balloon at constant pressure has a volume of 120 mL at −123°C. What is its volume at 27.0°C?
   - (A) 60.0 mL
   - (C) 26.5 mL
   - (B) 240.0 mL
   - (D) 546 mL

❶ Analyze

Use a knowns and unknown table to organize the temperature and volume data. You do not have to worry about the pressure because it does not change.

Which gas law relates temperature and volume? That's right, Charles's law. This law states that an increase in temperature will cause a similar increase in volume.

Knowns	Unknown
$V_1 = 120$ mL	$V_2 = ?$
$T_1 = -123°C$	
$T_2 = 27.0°C$	

❷ Solve

For Question 1, you do not need the expression for Charles's law. You just need to figure out how the temperature changed. Then you can apply what you find to the volume.

To begin, change the temperatures in °C to K by adding 273. Note that one of the temperatures is a negative number.

T_2 is twice as large as T_1. Because temperature and volume have a direct relationship, V_2 should be twice as large as V_1. Multiply V_1 by 2 to find V_2.

$-123°C + 273 = 150$ K

$27.0°C + 273 =$ _____

120 mL $\times 2 =$ _____

❸ Choose an Answer

Look at the answer choices. Do any of the choices match your answer? The correct answer is B.

Now you try it.

A gas in a closed container with a constant volume has a pressure of 104 kPa at −123°C. What is its pressure at 27.0°C?
   - (A) 22.8 kPa
   - (C) 208 kPa
   - (B) 52.0 kPa
   - (D) 473 kPa

Name _____ Class _____ Date _____

Use the drawing to answer Question 11. The key words have been highlighted for you.

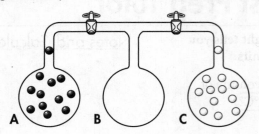

11. Bulb A and Bulb C contain different gases. Bulb B contains no gas. If the valves between the bulbs are opened, how will the particles of gas be distributed when the system reaches equilibrium? Assume none of the particles are in the tubes that connect the bulbs.

❶ **Analyze**

How many particles are in Bulb A before the valves are opened? How many particles are in Bulb B?

Bulb A = 12 particles

Bulb B = _____

Gases move from areas of higher concentration to areas of lower concentration. When the valves are opened, the gas in Bulb A will move toward Bulbs B and C. Where will the gas in Bulb C move toward?

The gas in Bulb C will move toward Bulbs B and A.

❷ **Solve**

The word *equilibrium* means "balanced" or "equal." The system will be at equilibrium when the number of particles is the same in each bulb. Divide the number of particles of each gas by the number of bulbs.

$$\frac{12 \text{ particles}}{3 \text{ bulbs}} = 4$$

❸ **Choose an Answer**

Read the question again. The question asks you to describe how the particles will be distributed, or divided, among the bulbs. Your answer should be a sentence.

Four black particles and four white particles will be in each bulb.

Now you try it.

If only the valve between Bulb A and B is opened, how will the particles of gas be distributed when the system reaches equilibrium?

_____

_____

If only the valve between Bulb B and C is opened, how will the particles of gas be distributed when the system reaches equilibrium?

_____

_____

_____

_____

More Practice Percent of Water in a Hydrate

Step-by-Step Practice

1. Calculate the percent by mass of water in borax, sodium tetraborate pentahydrate ($Na_2B_4O_7 \cdot 5H_2O$).

❶ Analyze List the known and the unknown.

Known	Unknown
formula of hydrate = $Na_2B_4O_7 \cdot 5H_2O$	percent by mass $H_2O = ?\%$

❷ Calculate Solve for the unknown.

Write the general equation for determining the percent by mass of water in a hydrate.

$$\text{Percent by mass } H_2O = \frac{\text{mass of water}}{\text{mass of hydrate}} \times 100\%$$

Calculate the mass of 5 mol of water.

$$\text{mass of 5 mol } H_2O = 5 \times ((2 \times 1.0 \text{ g}) + (1 \times 16.0 \text{ g}))$$
$$= 90.0 \text{ g}$$

Calculate the mass of 1 mol of $Na_2B_4O_7$.

$$\text{mass of 1 mol of } Na_2B_4O_7 = (2 \times 23.0) + (4 \times 10.8) + (7 \times 16.0)$$
$$= 201.2 \text{ g}$$

Calculate the mass of 1 mol of the hydrate $Na_2B_4O_7 \cdot 5H_2O$.

$$\text{mass of 1 mol of } Na_2B_4O_7 \cdot 5H_2O = 201.2 \text{ g} + 90.0 \text{ g}$$
$$= 291.2 \text{ g}$$

Substitute the values into the equation and solve.

$$\text{Percent by mass } H_2O = \frac{\text{mass of 5 mol } H_2O}{\text{mass of 1 mol } Na_2B_4O_7 \cdot 5 H_2O} \times 100\%$$

$$= \frac{90.0 \text{ g}}{291.2 \text{ g}} \times 100\% = 30.9\%$$

❸ Evaluate Does the result make sense?

The mass of the water in the hydrate is slightly less than a third of the total mass of the compound, so a result slightly less than 33 percent makes sense.

....

2. Drywall is made from gypsum, calcium sulfate dihydrate. What is the percent by mass of water in gypsum?

❶ Analyze List the known and the unknown.

Known	Unknown
formula of hydrate = $CaSO_4 \cdot 2H_2O$	percent by mass $H_2O = ?\%$

❷ Calculate **Solve for the unknown.**

Find the mass of the hydrate and the mass of the water in the hydrate.

molar mass of water in the hydrate = ____ × _____ = _____

molar mass of $CaSO_4$ = _____ + _____ + ____ × _____

= _____

molar mass of hydrate = _____ + _____ = _____

Calculate the percent by mass of water in gypsum.

Percent by mass $H_2O = \dfrac{\text{_____}}{\text{mass of 1 mol } CaSO_4 \cdot 2\,H_2O} \times 100\%$

$= \dfrac{\text{_____}}{\text{_____}} \times 100\% = $ _____

❸ Evaluate **Does the result make sense?**

The mass of the water is about _____ the mass of the _____, so a result close to ____ percent makes sense.

On Your Own

3. Cobalt(II) chloride changes color when exposed to water and is used as an indicator of humidity. Calculate the percent by mass of water in cobalt(II) chloride hexahydrate ($CoCl_2 \cdot 6H_2O$).

4. One of the solutions used to develop photographs taken with film cameras is sodium thiosulfate pentahydrate. Calculate the percent by mass of water in sodium thiosulfate pentahydrate ($Na_2S_2O_3 \cdot 5H_2O$).

15 Standardized Test Prep Tutor

Use the atomic windows to answer Question 4. The highlighted words describe an action. You are being asked to find the result of that action.

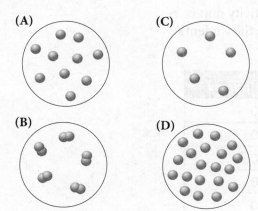

(A)

(C)

(B)

(D)

4. Atomic window A represents solute particles in a given volume of solution. Which window represents the solute particles in the same volume of solution when the amount of solvent is doubled?

The question is asking how the number of solute particles will change in a solution with twice as much solvent but the same total volume.

The concentration of solute particles in the solution will decrease because there are less solute particles in a greater amount of solvent. For a solution to have the same total volume with double the solvent, there must be half as many solute particles.

The first window has 10 solute particles.

You need a window with 5 solute particles.

The correct answer is Window C.

Now you try it.

Use the atomic windows in Question 4 to answer the following question.

Atomic window A represents solute particles in a given volume of solution. Which window represents the solute particles in the same volume of solution when the amount of solvent is cut in half? Explain your answer.

_____

_____

_____

_____

Use the description and the data table to answer Questions 5–7.

A student measured the conductivity of six aqueous solutions. Each solution had equal concentrations of solute. Solutes that produce a similar amount of particles when they dissociate into ions will have similar conductivity values. The magnitude of the conductivity value is proportional to the number of ions in the solution. The SI conductivity unit is the microsiemens/cm (μS/cm). The table gives the student's results.

Solution	Conductivity (μS/cm)
Potassium chloride, KCl	2050
Aluminum chloride, $AlCl_3$	4500
Calcium chloride, $CaCl_2$	3540
Sodium hydroxide, NaOH	2180
Ethanol, C_2H_6O	0
Magnesium bromide, $MgBr_2$	3490

You will be shown how to solve Questions 5 and 6. Then you will solve Question 7 on your own.

5. Why does the ethanol solution have zero conductivity?

   Look at the compounds listed in the table. How is ethanol different from the others? Ethanol is not an ionic compound. Ethanol molecules do not dissociate in water.

   An ethanol solution has no ions to conduct an electric current.

6. Explain why two pairs of conducting solutions have similar conductivities.

   Find the pairs of solutions that have similar conductivities.

   Pair 1: KCl and NaOH   Pair 2: $CaCl_2$ and $MgBr_2$

   List the ions that form when each solute dissolves.

   KCl: K^+ and Cl^- $CaCl_2$: Ca^+ and two Cl^+ ions

   NaOH: Na^+ OH^- $MgBr_2$: Mg^{2+} and two Br^- ions

   KCl and NaOH each contain two ions. $CaCl_2$ and $MgBr_2$ each contain three ions.

   The pairs have similar conductivities because their solutions contain the same number of ions.

   Now you try it.

7. The $AlCl_3$ solution has a conductivity that is about twice that of the KCl solution. Explain. *Hint:* Consider the number of ions available to carry an electric current in each solution.

   _____

   _____

   _____

Interpret Graphs Solubility and Temperature

Preview the Graph

This line graph shows the relationship between solubility and temperature for six solid substances. The chemical symbol for each substance is above the line that shows the solubility of the substance. Describe the line that shows the solubility of potassium nitrate (KNO_3).

_____

_____

_____

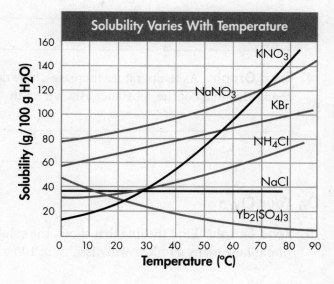

Solubility is the variable on the *y*-axis. What are the units for solubility?

_____

What is the variable on the *x*-axis? What happens to this variable as you move from left to right across the graph?

_____

_____

Analyze the Graph

Now you are ready to answer some more questions. As you read the questions:

▶ Highlight key words.
▶ Circle numbers and units.

Use the first question as an example.

1. **Read Graphs** Find the line that shows the solubility of sodium nitrate ($NaNO_3$). About how many grams of $NaNO_3$ will dissolve in 100 g of water at 10°C?

_____

> **Try it!** Place your finger on the x-axis at 10°C. Move it up to the line for $NaNO_3$. Then move your finger to the y-axis to find the solubility.

2. **Compare** Out of the six substances on the graph, which has the highest solubility at 80°C?

_____

> **Try it!** Find the line that is closest to the top of the graph at 80°C.

3. Compare Which substance has the smallest change in solubility when temperature changes? How can you tell?

_____

_____

_____

> **Try it!** Look for the line that looks flat instead of curving up or down. A flat line shows that solubility doesn't change as temperature changes.

4. Read Graphs As temperature increases, how does solubility change for most of the substances shown on the graph?

_____

_____

> **Try it!** Look to see whether most of the lines curve upward or downward as temperature increases.

On Your Own

5. Read Graphs Find the line that shows the solubility of potassium bromide (KBr). About how many g of KBr will dissolve in 100 g of water at 40°C?

_____

6. Read Graphs Which three substances have similar solubility at 28°C?

_____

7. Read Graphs Which substance is less soluble at higher temperatures than at lower temperatures?

_____

8. Compare Look at the lines showing the solubility of sodium nitrate ($NaNO_3$) and potassium nitrate (KNO_3). Which of these two substances is more soluble at 65°C? Which is more soluble at 75°C?

_____

_____

9. Apply Concepts Could you make a supersaturated solution of ytterbium sulfate, $Yb_2(SO_4)_3$, by making a saturated solution at 60°C and then letting it cool without stirring it? Explain. *Hint:* A supersaturated solution contains more solute than a saturated solution.

_____

_____

More Practice Calculating Molarity

Lesson 16.2

Step-by-Step Practice

1. A solution contains 35.4 g of platinum(IV) chloride ($PtCl_4$) in 975 mL of solution. What is the molarity of the solution?

❶ Analyze List the knowns and the unknown.

Knowns	Unknown
mass of $PtCl_4$ = 35.4 g	molarity = ?M
volume of solution = 975 mL	
molar mass of $PtCl_4$ = 336.9 g/mol	

❷ Solve Solve for the unknown.

Molarity equals moles of solute divided by liters of solution. You will need to know the moles of $PtCl_4$ and the volume of the solution in liters in order to calculate molarity.

$$M = \frac{\text{moles of solute}}{\text{liters of solution}}$$

Use the molar mass of platinum(IV) chloride to convert grams of $PtCl_4$ to moles of $PtCl_4$.

$$35.4 \text{ g } PtCl_4 \times \frac{1 \text{ mol } PtCl_4}{336.9 \text{ g } PtCl_4} = 0.105 \text{ mol } PtCl_4$$

Convert the volume of the solution from milliliters to liters using a conversion factor.

$$975 \text{ mL} \times \frac{1 \text{ L}}{1000 \text{ mL}} = 0.975 \text{ L}$$

Substitute the number of moles of $PtCl_4$ and the liters of solution into the formula for molarity. Then solve the equation.

$$M = \frac{\text{moles of solute}}{\text{liters of solution}}$$

$$= \frac{0.105 \text{ mol } PtCl_4}{0.975 \text{ L solution}} = 0.108M$$

❸ Evaluate Does the result make sense?

The volume of solution is very close to 1 L, so the answer should be very close to the number of moles of $PtCl_4$. The answer is correct to 3 significant figures.

2. Silver nitrate ($AgNO_3$) is used to make the reflective surface of some mirrors. One silver nitrate solution contains 1.167 g $AgNO_3$ in 0.175 L of solution. What is the molarity of this solution?

❶ Analyze List the knowns and the unknown.

Knowns	Unknown
mass of $AgNO_3$ = _____	molarity = ?M
volume of solution = _____	
molar mass of $AgNO_3$ = 169.9 g/mol	

❷ Calculate Solve for the unknown.

Use the molar mass of silver nitrate to convert grams of $AgNO_3$ to moles of $AgNO_3$.

$$\_\_\_\_ \text{ g } AgNO_3 \times \frac{1 \text{ mol } AgNO_3}{169.9 \text{ g } AgNO_3}$$

$$= _____ \text{ mol } AgNO_3$$

Substitute the number of moles of $AgNO_3$ and the liters of solution into the formula for molarity. Then solve the equation.

$$M = \frac{\text{moles of solute}}{\text{liters of solution}}$$

$$= \frac{_____}{_____} = _____$$

❸ Evaluate Does the result make sense?

How much larger is 1 L than the volume of the silver nitrate solution? _____

How much larger is the molarity than the number of moles of solute? _____

On Your Own

3. A solution has a volume of 0.709 L and contains 7.95 mol of ammonium nitrate (NH_4NO_3). What is the molarity of the solution?

4. Lead(II) acetate, $Pb(C_2H_3O_2)_2$, is one of a small number of very soluble lead compounds. What is the molarity of a solution containing 27.8 g lead(II) acetate in 374 mL of solution? The molar mass of $Pb(C_2H_3O_2)_2$ = 325.3 g/mol.

More Practice Moles of Solute in a Solution

Lesson 16.2

Step-by-Step Practice

1. Citric acid is added to some food to keep it from spoiling. How many moles of solute are in 0.375 L of a 0.15M citric acid solution?

❶ **Analyze** List the knowns and the unknown.

Knowns	Unknown
concentration (M) = 0.15M citric acid	moles of solute = ? mol
volume (V) = 0.375 L	

❷ **Calculate** Solve for the unknown.

Write the equation for moles of solute.

moles of solute = $M \times V$

Substitute the knowns into the equation and then solve.

moles of solute = $\dfrac{0.15 \text{ mol citric acid}}{1 \cancel{L}} \times 0.375 \cancel{L}$

= 0.056 mol citric acid

❸ **Evaluate** Does the result make sense?

The volume of solution is slightly greater than one third of a liter. So the moles should be slightly greater than one third of 0.15, or 0.5. The answer is correct to two significant figures.

....

2. How many moles of solute are in 1.25 L of 3.75M of phosphoric acid, H_3PO_4?

❶ **Analyze** List the knowns and the unknown.

Knowns	Unknown
concentration (M) =	moles of solute = ? mol
volume (V) =	

❷ **Calculate** Solve for the unknown.

Substitute the knowns into the equation and then solve.

moles of solute = ——————— ×

=

③ Evaluate **Does the result make sense?**

_____

_____

On Your Own

3. Tin(II) fluoride (SnF_2) is used in some toothpastes to help prevent cavities. How many moles of tin(II) fluoride are in 6.26 L of a $0.00197M$ SnF_2 solution?

4. In a chemistry lab, a solution of sodium hydroxide (NaOH) is labeled $3.975M$. How many moles of NaOH are in 226 mL of this solution? *Hint:* 1 L = 1000 mL.

5. Magnesium sulfate ($MgSO_4$) is found in bath salts. How many moles of magnesium sulfate are in 1.47 L of a $0.289M$ solution of $MgSO_4$?

More Practice Using Molality

Step-by-Step Practice

1. How many grams of ammonium chloride (NH_4Cl) must be dissolved in 500 g of water to produce a $1.00m$ NH_4Cl solution?

   ❶ **Analyze** List the knowns and the unknown.

Knowns	Unknown
mass of water, or solvent = 500 g	mass of solute = ? g NH_4Cl
molality = 1.00m	
molar mass of NH_4Cl = 53.5 g/mol	

   ❷ **Calculate** Solve for the unknown.

   Molality is the number of moles of solute per kilogram of solvent. So you need to use a conversion factor to change the mass of the water from grams to kilograms.

   $$\text{mass of water} = 500 \text{ g} \times \frac{1 \text{ kg}}{1000 \text{ g}}$$
   $$= 0.500 \text{ kg H}_2\text{O}$$

   Multiply the mass of the water in kilograms by the molality to find the moles of the solute, NH_4Cl.

   $$\text{moles of solute} = 0.500 \text{ kg H}_2\text{O} \times \frac{1.00 \text{ mol NH}_4\text{Cl}}{1.000 \text{ kg H}_2\text{O}}$$
   $$= 0.500 \text{ mol NH}_4\text{Cl}$$

   Multiply the moles of NH_4Cl by the molar mass of NH_4Cl to find the mass of the solute.

   $$\text{moles of solute} = 0.500 \text{ mol NH}_4\text{Cl} \times \frac{53.5 \text{ g NH}_4\text{Cl}}{1 \text{ mol NH}_4\text{Cl}}$$
   $$= 26.8 \text{ g NH}_4\text{Cl}$$

   ❸ **Evaluate** Does the result make sense?

   A 1 molal NH_4Cl solution would have 53.5 g of NH_4Cl dissolved in 1000 g of water. This solution uses only 500 g of water, so you only need one half of the solute, or about 26.8 g.

2. A 0.50 molal solution is made by dissolving 46.0 g magnesium bromide ($MgBr_2$) in water. How many kilograms of water are needed to make this solution?

❶ Analyze List the knowns and the unknown.

Knowns	Unknown
mass of solute = _____	mass of water = ? kg H_2O
molality = _____	
molar mass of $MgBr_2$ = 184.1 g/mol	

❷ Calculate Solve for the unknown.

To solve this problem, first, multiply the mass of the solute by the molar mass of $MgBr_2$ to find the moles of $MgBr_2$.

$$\text{moles of solute} = \times \frac{1 \text{ mol } MgBr_2}{184.1 \text{ g } MgBr_2}$$

$$= \underline{} \text{ mol } MgBr_2$$

Then, multiply the moles of solute by the molality to find the mass of the water.

$$\text{mass of water} = \times \frac{1.000 \text{ kg } H_2O}{0.50 \text{ mol } MgBr_2}$$

$$= \underline{} \text{ kg } H_2O$$

❸ Evaluate Does the result make sense?

A $1m$ $MgBr_2$ solution would have 184.1 g $MgBr_2$ dissolved in 1.000 kg of water. A $0.50m$ solution would have 92.1 g $MgBr_2$ dissolved in 1.000 kg of water. How much water would you need for a $0.50m$ solution made with 46.0 g of solute?

_____

On Your Own

3. How many grams of sodium dichromate ($Na_2Cr_2O_7$) are needed to make a $0.500m$ solution using 750.0 g of water? The molar mass of $Na_2Cr_2O_7$ is 262.0 g/mol.

More Practice Freezing Point Depression of a Solution Lesson 16.4

Step-by-Step Practice

1. What is the freezing point depression of a solution containing 100 g of ethanol (C_2H_5OH) in 0.750 kg of water?

   ❶ Analyze **List the knowns and the unknown.**

Knowns	Unknown
mass of solute = 100 g C_2H_5OH	$\Delta T_f = ?°C$
mass of solvent = 0.750 kg H_2O	
K_f for H_2O = 1.86°C/m	
molar mass of C_2H_5OH = 46.0 g/mol	

   ❷ Calculate **Solve for the unknown.**

   You need to know the molality of the solution to find its freezing point depression. First, use the molar mass of ethanol to convert the mass of solute to moles.

   $$\text{moles of solute} = 100 \text{ g } C_2H_5OH \times \frac{1 \text{ mol } C_2H_5OH}{46.0 \text{ g } C_2H_5OH}$$
   $$= 2.17 \text{ mol } C_2H_5OH$$

   Then calculate the molality of the solution.

   $$\text{molality} = \frac{\text{moles of solute}}{\text{kg solvent}}$$
   $$= \frac{2.17 \text{ mol } C_2H_5OH}{0.750 \text{ kg } H_2O} = 2.89m$$

   Substitute known values into the freezing point depression equation and solve.

   $$\Delta T_f = K_f \times m = 1.86°C/m \times 2.89m = 5.38°C$$

   ❸ Evaluate **Does the result make sense?**

   A 1 molal solution reduces the freezing temperature by a little less than 2°C. A solution that is close to 3 molal would reduce the freezing temperature by a little less than 6°C. The result is correct to three significant figures.

2. What is the freezing point depression of a solution resulting from 200 grams of trichloromethane ($CHCl_3$) added to 0.90 kg of benzene?

① Analyze List the knowns and the unknown.

Knowns	Unknown
mass of solute = _____	_____
mass of solvent = _____	
K_f for benzene = 5.12°C/m	
molar mass of $CHCl_3$ = 119.5 g/mol	

② Calculate Solve for the unknown.

Use the molar mass of $CHCl_3$ to convert the mass of solute to moles.

$$\text{moles of solute} = \_\_\_\_\_ \text{ g } CHCl_3 \times \frac{1 \text{ mol } CHCl_3}{119.5 \text{ g } CHCl_3}$$

$$= \_\_\_\_\_ \text{ mol } CHCl_3$$

Determine the molality of the solution.

$$\text{molality} = \frac{1.67 \text{ mol } CHCl_3}{0.90 \text{ kg benzene}} = _____$$

Substitute known values into the freezing point depression equation and solve.

$$\Delta T_f = 5.12°C/m \times _____ = _____$$

③ Evaluate Does the result make sense?

_____

_____

On Your Own

3. What is the freezing point depression of a solution containing 250 grams of glycerin ($C_3H_8O_3$) in 1.25 kg of ethanol? Molar mass of $C_3H_8O_3$ = 92.0 g/mol; K_f for ethanol = 1.99°C/m.

4. What freezing point depression will result when 20.0 g of toluene (C_7H_8) is dissolved in 0.150 kilograms of acetic acid? molality = 1.45m; K_f for acetic acid = 3.90°C/m.

16 Standardized Test Prep Tutor

Use the atomic windows to answer Questions 7–9. The windows show water and two aqueous solutions with different concentrations. Black spheres represent solute particles; gray spheres represent water.

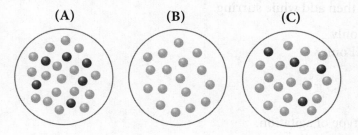

(A)   (B)   (C)

7. Which solution has the highest vapor pressure?

8. Which solution has the lowest vapor pressure?

9. Which solution has the lowest boiling point?

Choose the window that answers each question correctly. Remember that water is not a solution, so window B can be ruled out for all three questions.

7. Which solution has the highest vapor pressure?

   Vapor pressure is high when many particles can escape from a liquid to become vapor. Solute particles decrease the number of solvent particles that can escape from a liquid. So the solution with the fewest solute particles would have the highest vapor pressure.

   Window C shows the solution with the highest vapor pressure.

8. Which solution has the lowest vapor pressure?

   Vapor pressure decreases as solute particles are added to a solution. So the solution with the most solute particles would have the lowest vapor pressure.

   Window A shows the solution with the lowest vapor pressure.

9. Which solution has the lowest boiling point?

   Boiling point increases as solute particles are added to a solution. So the solution with the fewest solute particles and highest vapor pressure would have the lowest boiling point.

   Window C shows the solution with the lowest boiling point.

   Now you try it.

   Which solution has the highest boiling point?

_____

_____

_____

Read the question and decide which of the statements labeled I, II, and III are correct. More than one statement may be correct. Then find the answer that describes your choice or choices.

10. Which of these actions will cause more sugar to dissolve in a saturated sugar water solution?

    I. Add more sugar while stirring.

    II. Add more sugar and then heat the solution.

    III. Grind the sugar to a powder and then add while stirring.

    (A) I only
    (B) II only
    (C) III only
    (D) I and II only
    (E) II and III only

❶ Analyze

Action I involves stirring, which is a type of agitation. Agitation causes sugar to dissolve more quickly.

Action II involves heating. Sugar dissolves more quickly when a solution is warmer. The solubility of sugar in water increases as the temperature of the water increases.

Action III involves changing the particle size of the sugar. Smaller particles dissolve faster, because they have more surface area.

❷ Solve

Actions I and III affect how quickly the sugar can dissolve. However, they cannot change the amount of sugar that will dissolve in a saturated solution.

Action II increases the amount of sugar that can dissolve in a saturated solution.

❸ Choose an Answer

Look at the answer choices. Find the answer choice that includes only Action II. The correct answer is B.

Now you try it.

Which of these actions will cause more carbon dioxide gas to be dissolved in a saturated soft drink solution?

    I. Add more carbon dioxide while agitating the solution.

    II. Add more carbon dioxide while cooling the solution.

    III. Add more carbon dioxide while increasing the pressure of the gas above the solution.

    (A) I only
    (B) II only
    (C) III only
    (D) I and II only
    (E) II and III only

Interpret Data

Specific Heats of Common Substances

Preview the Table

The table lists the specific heats of some common substances. The names of the substances appear in the first column.

Two names in the Substances column refer to the same compound. Circle these two names in the table. Then write the corresponding formula for each name.

_____

_____

Specific Heats of Some Common Substances		
Substance	Specific heat	
	J/(g·°C)	cal/(g·°C)
Liquid water	4.18	1.00
Ethanol	2.4	0.58
Steam	1.9	0.45
Chloroform	0.96	0.23
Aluminum	0.90	0.21
Silver	0.24	0.057

For each substance, the specific heat is given in two different units. What are the units used for specific heat?

_____

_____

Specific heat is the amount of heat required to raise the temperature of 1 gram of a substance by 1°C. Look at the units used for specific heat. What does the symbol "J" represent? What does the symbol "cal" represent? Which one is the SI unit of energy?

_____

_____

Analyze the Table

Now you are ready to answer some more questions. As you read the questions:

► Highlight key words.
► Circle numbers and units.

Use the first question as an example.

1. Read Tables What is the specific heat of steam in J/(g·°C)?

_____

Try it! Find the row for steam. Then read across to find its specific heat in the column labeled J/(g·°C).

2. Identify Which substance in the table has the highest specific heat? Which substance has the lowest specific heat?

_____

_____

> **Try it!** Find the highest and lowest values in one of the specific heat columns. Then find the corresponding substances.

3. Compare Which substance has a lower specific heat—liquid water or steam?

_____

_____

> **Try it!** Locate the rows for liquid water and steam. Find the specific heat for each substance, and then compare the values.

On Your Own

4. Read Tables Which substance has a specific heat of 0.58 cal/(g·°C)?

_____

5. Read Tables What is the specific heat of chloroform in J/(g·°C)? In cal/(g·°C)?

_____

_____

6. Compare Which metal has a higher specific heat—aluminum or silver?

_____

7. Interpret Data How many joules of heat are required to raise the temperature of 1 g of aluminum by 1°C?

_____

8. Calculate You can convert between calories and joules using the following relationship:

$$1 \text{ J} = 0.2390 \text{ cal}$$

Show how to convert the specific heat of liquid water in units of J/(g·°C) to units of cal/(g·°C). *Hint:* Use the equation above to write a conversion factor that allows you to convert from J to cal.

More Practice Calculating Specific Heat

Lesson 17.1

Step-by-Step Practice

1. The temperature of a granite rock with a mass of 215 g increases from 24.0°C to 35.5°C when the rock absorbs 1950 J of heat. What is the specific heat of granite?

❶ Analyze List the knowns and unknown.

Knowns	Unknown
$m_{granite} = 215$ g	$C_{granite} = ?$ J/(g·°C)
$T_f = 35.5°C$	
$T_i = 24.0°C$	
$q = 1950$ J	

❷ Calculate Solve for the unknown.

Before using the equation for specific heat, you must find the change in temperature, ΔT.

$$\Delta T = T_f - T_i = 35.5°C - 24.0°C = 11.5°C$$

Write the equation for specific heat.

$$C_{granite} = \frac{q}{m_{granite} \times \Delta T}$$

Substitute the knowns into the equation and solve.

$$C_{granite} = \frac{1950 \text{ J}}{215 \text{ g} \times 11.5°C} = 0.789 \text{ J/(g·°C)}$$

❸ Evaluate Does the result make sense?

The calculated value of 0.789 J/(g·°C) is higher than many metals but lower than the specific heat of water, which is 4.18 J/(g·°C). The result seems reasonable.

2. A 15.0-g block of zinc is immersed in boiling water. The temperature of the block increases from 22.0°C to 100.0°C as it absorbs 459 J of heat. What is the specific heat of zinc?

❶ Analyze List the knowns and unknown.

Knowns	Unknown
$m_{zinc} = 15.0$ g	$C_{zinc} = ?$ J/(g·°C)
$T_f = $ _____	
$T_i = $ _____	
$q = $ _____	

❷ Calculate **Solve for the unknown.**

Find the change in temperature, ΔT.

$$\Delta T = T_f - T_i$$

$$\Delta T = \underline{\hspace{1.5cm}} - \underline{\hspace{1.5cm}} = \underline{\hspace{1.5cm}}$$

Write the equation for specific heat.

$$C_{zinc} = \frac{}{m_{zinc} \times}$$

Substitute the knowns into the equation and solve.

$$C_{zinc} = \frac{}{15.0 \text{ g} \times} =$$

❸ Evaluate **Does the result make sense?**

The specific heat of common metals is within the range 0.1 J/(g·°C) to 2.0 J/(g·°C). Is your calculated answer within this range? _____

On Your Own

3. A 6.5-g block of aluminum absorbs 9.0×10^2 J of heat when its temperature increases by 150°C. What is the specific heat of aluminum?

4. A 245-g drinking glass is left outside on a hot day. Its temperature increases from 21.5°C to 31.5°C as it absorbs 2060 J of heat. What is the specific heat of the glass?

5. A musician's brass trumpet has a mass of 1950 g. During an outdoor concert on a hot summer day, the trumpet's temperature increases from 20.5°C to 28.0°C. If the trumpet absorbed 5.37×10^3 J of heat, what is its specific heat?

More Practice Calculating Enthalpy Change

Lesson 17.2

Step-by-Step Practice

1. How many kilojoules of heat are produced when 2.30 mol CH_4 burns in excess O_2?

$$CH_4(g) + 2O_2(g) \longrightarrow CO_2(g) + 2H_2O(l) + 890 \text{ kJ}$$

❶ Analyze List the knowns and unknown.

Knowns	Unknown
amount of CH_4 = 2.30 mol	ΔH = ? kJ for 2.30 mol
ΔH = −890 kJ for 1 mol	

❷ Calculate Solve for the unknown.

Use the thermochemical equation to write a conversion factor that will allow you to convert from moles of CH_4 to kJ of heat.

$$\frac{-890 \text{ kJ}}{1 \text{ mol } CH_4(g)}$$

Solve for ΔH by multiplying the given amount of CH_4 by the conversion factor.

$$\Delta H = 2.30 \text{ mol } CH_4(g) \times \frac{-890 \text{ kJ}}{1 \text{ mol } CH_4(g)}$$
$$= -2.05 \times 10^3 \text{ kJ}$$

The reaction produces 2.05×10^3 kJ of heat.

❸ Evaluate Does the result make sense?

Burning 1 mol $CH_4(g)$ produces 890 kJ of heat. Burning 2 mol $CH_4(g)$ produces 2 × 890 kJ = 1780 kJ, or 1.78×10^3 kJ. This estimate is close to the calculated answer of 2.05×10^3 kJ.

....

2. Calculate the amount of heat required to decompose 7.03 mol $CaCO_3(s)$.

$$CaCO_3(s) + 176 \text{ kJ} \longrightarrow CaO(s) + CO_2(g)$$

❶ Analyze List the knowns and unknown.

Knowns	Unknown
amount of $CaCO_3$ = 7.03 mol	ΔH = ? kJ for 7.03 mol
ΔH = _____ for 1 mol	

❷ Calculate Solve for the unknown.

Use the thermochemical equation to write a conversion
factor that will allow you to convert from moles of $CaCO_3$
to kJ of heat. The units for the conversion factor have been
placed for you. Fill in the correct numbers.

$$\frac{kJ}{mol\ CaCO_3(s)}$$

Solve for ΔH by multiplying the given amount
of $CaCO_3$ by the conversion factor.

$\Delta H =$ _____ $\times \dfrac{kJ}{mol\ CaCO_3(s)}$

$=$

❸ Evaluate Does the result make sense?

The decomposition of 1 mol $CaCO_3(s)$ requires _____ of heat.

Is your calculated answer about 7 times this amount? _____

On Your Own

3. Sulfur reacts with oxygen gas to form sulfur dioxide. The reaction is exothermic.
How much energy is released when 4.05 mol S reacts with an excess of O_2?

$$S(s) + O_2(g) \longrightarrow SO_2(g) + 297\ kJ$$

4. Calculate the enthalpy change when 2.0 mol NH_3 reacts with an excess of O_2 according
to the following equation.

$$4NH_3(g) + 7O_2(g) \longrightarrow 4NO_2(g) + 6H_2O(l) + 1131\ kJ$$

5. How many kilojoules of heat are produced by burning 9.1 g of acetylene (C_2H_2)?

$$2C_2H_2(g) + 5O_2(g) \longrightarrow 4CO_2(g) + 2H_2O(l) + 2600\ kJ$$

More Practice Heat in Changes of State

Lesson 17.3

Step-by-Step Practice

1. How many grams of ice will melt at 0°C when 3.23 kJ of heat is added? The molar heat of fusion for water is 6.01 kJ/mol.

❶ Analyze List the knowns and the unknown.

Knowns	Unknown
$\Delta H_{fus} = 6.01$ kJ/mol	$m_{ice} = ?$ g
$\Delta H = 3.23$ kJ	
$T_i = T_f = 0°C$	

❷ Calculate Solve for the unknown.

To solve this problem, you need two conversion factors, one that relates heat to moles and one that relates moles to grams.

Express ΔH_{fus} as a conversion factor. Express the molar mass of ice as a conversion factor.

$$\frac{1 \text{ mol } H_2O(s)}{6.01 \text{ kJ}} \qquad \frac{18.0 \text{ g } H_2O(s)}{1 \text{ mol } H_2O(s)}$$

Multiply the amount of heat added by both conversion factors. Then solve the equation.

$$m_{ice} = \frac{3.23 \text{ kJ}}{6.01 \text{ kJ}} \frac{1 \text{ mol } H_2O(s)}{} \times \frac{18.0 \text{ g } H_2O(s)}{1 \text{ mol } H_2O(s)}$$

$$m_{ice} = 9.67 \text{ g}$$

❸ Evaluate Does the result make sense?

To melt 1 mol of ice, 6.01 kJ of energy is needed. About half this amount of heat is available, so about 0.5 mol of ice, or about 9 g, should melt.

....

2. How many kilojoules of heat are absorbed when 23.8 g of ethanol vaporizes at its normal boiling point, 78.3°C? For ethanol, the molar heat of vaporization is 0.90 kJ/mol. The molar mass of ethanol is 46.07 g/mol.

❶ Analyze List the knowns and the unknown.

Knowns	Unknown
$\Delta H_{vap} =$ _____	$\Delta H = ?$ kJ
$m_{ethanol} =$ _____	
molar mass = _____	

❷ Calculate Solve for the unknown.

Use the molar mass of ethanol to write a conversion factor that will convert grams of ethanol to moles of ethanol. You also need to express ΔH_{vap} as a conversion factor.

$$\frac{1 \text{ mol } C_2H_6O(l)}{} \qquad \frac{}{1 \text{ mol } C_2H_6O(l)}$$

Multiply the mass of ethanol in grams by both conversion factors.

$$\Delta H = \times \frac{}{} \times \frac{}{}$$

$$\Delta H = \underline{}$$

❸ Evaluate Does the result make sense?

_____

_____

_____

On Your Own

3. How many grams of ice at 0°C will melt if you add 2.18 kJ of heat? The molar heat of fusion for water is 6.01 kJ/mol.

4. Calculate the enthalpy change when 1.26 g of oxygen gas condenses at its normal boiling point. The molar heat of vaporization for oxygen is 6.82 kJ/mol.

5. A beaker contains 5.80 g of ice. If you add 0.615 kJ of heat, how many grams of the ice will stay frozen? *Hint:* First find how many grams will melt.

Interpret Graphs Heating Curve for Water

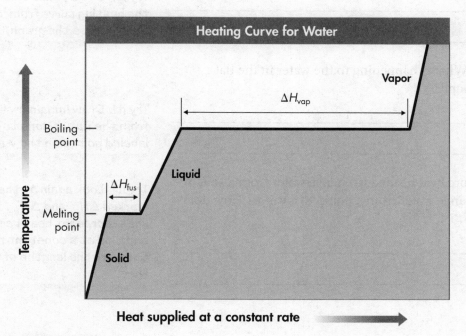

Preview the Graph

The graph shows how the state of water changes as heat is added or removed. Notice the labels for the solid, liquid, and vapor (gas) states. The heating curve referred to in the title is represented by the heavy black line.

Look at the y-axis. The graph uses an arrow pointing up instead of specific units to show that the temperature is increasing. What two temperature points are marked on the y-axis?

_____

Look at the x-axis. The variable is heat supplied. When you read the graph from left to right, the heat supplied increases at a constant rate. When you read the graph from right to left, the heat supplied decreases at a constant rate.

Find the symbol ΔH_{fus} on the graph. It represents the molar heat of fusion, or the amount of heat needed to melt a mole of a given solid. Find the symbol ΔH_{vap}. What does this symbol represent?

_____

Analyze the Graph

Now you are ready to answer some more questions. As you read the questions:

▶ Highlight key words.

▶ Circle numbers and units.

Use the first question as an example.

1. **Describe** How does the heating curve change as you move from left to right across the graph?

_____

_____

> **Try it!** Use a pencil to trace the heating curve from left to right across the graph.

2. **Read Graphs** What is happening to the water in the flat regions of the graph?

_____

_____

> **Try it!** Draw imaginary lines from the flat regions to the labeled points on the y-axis.

3. **Compare** Is more heat needed to change water from a solid to a liquid or to change water from a liquid to a vapor? How do you know?

_____

_____

> **Try it!** Look again at the lines marked ΔH_{fus} and ΔH_{vap}. The lines represent heat being supplied at a constant rate. Compare the lengths of the lines.

On Your Own

4. **Read Graphs** What happens to the temperature when water changes from a vapor to a liquid?

_____

5. **Compare** Is more heat removed when a mole of water changes from a vapor to a liquid or when a mole of water changes from a liquid to a solid? Explain.

_____

_____

6. **Predict** A student records the temperature of water as it changes from a vapor to a liquid to a solid. Then the student graphs the data. Describe how this cooling curve would look.

_____

_____

7. **Make a Generalization** What happens to the temperature of a substance during a phase change?

_____

_____

More Practice Standard Heat of Reaction

Step-by-Step Practice

1. Calculate the standard heat of reaction ($\Delta H°$) for the formation of sulfur trioxide from sulfur dioxide and oxygen gas. Use the following standard heats of formation:

$$\Delta H_f° SO_2(g) = -296.8 \text{ kJ/mol}$$

$$\Delta H_f° SO_3(g) = -395.7 \text{ kJ/mol}$$

❶ **Analyze** List the knowns and unknown.

Knowns	Unknown
$\Delta H_f° SO_2(g) =$ -296.8 kJ/mol	$\Delta H° = ?$ kJ
$\Delta H_f° O_2(g) =$ 0 kJ/mol	
$\Delta H_f° SO_3(g) =$ -395.7 kJ/mol	

❷ **Calculate** Solve for the unknown.

Write the equation for the standard heat of reaction.

$$\Delta H° = \Delta H°(\text{products}) - \Delta H°(\text{reactants})$$

Write the balanced chemical equation.

$$2SO_2(g) + O_2(g) \longrightarrow 2SO_3(g)$$

Find $\Delta H_f°$ of the reactants.

$$\Delta H°(\text{reactants}) = \left[2 \text{ mol } SO_2(g) \times \frac{-296.8 \text{ kJ/mol}}{1 \text{ mol } SO_2(g)} \right]$$
$$+ \left[1 \text{ mol } O_2(g) \times \frac{0 \text{ kJ/mol}}{1 \text{ mol } O_2(g)} \right]$$

$$\Delta H°(\text{reactants}) = -593.6 \text{ kJ/mol}$$

Find $\Delta H_f°$ of the product.

$$\Delta H°(\text{product}) = 2 \text{ mol } SO_3(g) \times \frac{-395.7 \text{ kJ/mol}}{1 \text{ mol } SO_3(g)}$$

$$\Delta H°(\text{product}) = -791.4 \text{ kJ/mol}$$

Substitute into the equation for $\Delta H°$ and solve.

$$\Delta H° = (-791.4 \text{ kJ/mol}) - (-593.6 \text{ kJ/mol})$$

$$\Delta H° = -197.8 \text{ kJ/mol}$$

❸ **Evaluate** Does the result make sense?

$\Delta H°$ is negative, so the reaction is exothermic.
The reaction releases heat.

2. What is the standard heat of reaction ($\Delta H°$) for the decomposition of $CaCO_3(s)$ into $CaO(s)$ and $CO_2(g)$? Use the following standard heats of formation:

$$\Delta H_f°CaCO_3(s) = -1207.0 \text{ kJ/mol}$$

$$\Delta H_f°CaO(s) = -635.1 \text{ kJ/mol}$$

$$\Delta H_f°CO_2(g) = -393.5 \text{ kJ/mol}$$

❶ **Analyze** List the knowns and unknown.

Knowns	Unknown
$\Delta H_f°CaCO_3(s) = -1207.0$ kJ/mol	$\Delta H° = ?$ kJ
$\Delta H_f°CaO(s) = $ _____	
$\Delta H_f°CO_2(g) = $ _____	

❷ **Calculate** Solve for the unknown.

Write the balanced chemical equation. $CaCO_3(s) \longrightarrow$ _____ + _____

Find $\Delta H_f°$ of the reactant. $\Delta H°$(reactant) = ____ mol $CaCO_3(s) \times \dfrac{}{1 \text{ mol } CaCO_3(s)}$

$\Delta H°$(reactant) = _____

Find $\Delta H_f°$ of the products. $\Delta H°$(products) = $\left[\text{____ mol } CaO(s) \times \dfrac{\text{kJ/mol}}{1 \text{ mol } CaO(s)} \right]$

$+ \left[\text{____ mol } CO_2(g) \times \dfrac{\text{kJ/mol}}{1 \text{ mol } CO_2(g)} \right]$

$\Delta H°$(products) = _____

Substitute into the equation for $\Delta H°$ and solve. $\Delta H° = \Delta H°$(products) $- \Delta H°$(reactant)

$\Delta H° = $ _____ $-$ _____

$\Delta H° = $ _____

❸ **Evaluate** Does the result make sense?

Is $\Delta H°$ positive or negative? _____

Is the reaction endothermic or exothermic? _____

17 Standardized Test Prep Tutor

Read the question. Circle numbers and units.

1. The ΔH_{fus} of ethanol (C_2H_6O) is 4.93 kJ/mol . How many kilojoules are required to melt 24.5 g of ethanol at its freezing point?
   (A) 2.63 kJ   (C) 9.27 kJ
   (B) 4.97 kJ   (D) 263 kJ

❶ Analyze

Use a knowns and unknowns table to organize the data. You do not have to worry about the temperature because it is constant during a phase change.

To determine the number of kilojoules, you need to find the relationship between the mass of ethanol and the molar mass of ethanol.

❷ Solve

To begin, use the periodic table to find the molar mass of ethanol.

Then use the molar mass to find the number of moles of ethanol.

To find the number of kilojoules, you need to multiply the number of moles by ΔH_{fus}. Notice that the answer choices vary greatly in value. So you can do an estimate to find the product.

❸ Choose an Answer

Look at the answer choices. Are any of the choices close to your estimated answer? The correct answer is A.

Now you try it.

The ΔH_{fus} of water (H_2O) is 6.02 kJ/mol. How much heat is needed to melt 37.0 g of water at its freezing point (0°C)?
   (A) 2.05 kJ   (C) 12.4 kJ
   (B) 8.07 kJ   (D) 223 kJ

Knowns	Unknown
ΔH_{fus} = 4.93 kJ/mol	molar mass of ethanol = ?
mass of ethanol = 24.5 g	moles of ethanol = ?
	number of kilojoules = ?

Molar mass C_2H_6O
= 2(12.0) + 6(1.0) + 16.0
= 46.0 g/mol

$24.5 \text{ g} \times \dfrac{1 \text{ mol } C_2H_6O}{46.0 \text{ g}}$
= 0.532 mol

Round 4.93 kJ/mol to 5.0 kJ/mol.

Round 0.532 mol to 0.50 mol.

$50 \dfrac{kJ}{mol} \times 0.50 \text{ mol} = $ _____

Use the graph and table to answer Questions 7–10.
Assume 1.00 mol of each substance.

Substance	Freezing point (K)	ΔH_{fus} (kJ/mol)	Boiling point (K)	ΔH_{vap} (kJ/mol)
Ammonia	195.3	5.66	239.7	23.3
Benzene	278.7	9.87	353.3	30.8
Methanol	175.5	3.22	337.2	35.2
Neon	24.5	0.33	27.1	1.76

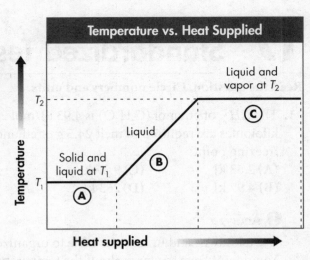

Temperature vs. Heat Supplied

You will be shown how to solve Questions 7 and 9.
Then you will solve Questions 8 and 10 on your own.

7. Calculate heat absorbed in region A for neon.

   Look at region A on the graph. In this region, a solid is melting at a constant temperature. The heat absorbed when a solid melts at a constant temperature is the molar heat of fusion. Find the molar heat of fusion for neon in the table.

   $\Delta H_{fus} = 0.33$ kJ/mol

9. Calculate heat absorbed in region B for methanol (CH_4O). [specific heat = 2.53 J/(g · °C)]

   Look at region B on the graph. In this region the temperature increases from the freezing point to the boiling point and methanol is a liquid. To calculate the heat absorbed by the liquid, first find ΔT for methanol.

   ΔT = boiling point – freezing point
   = 337.2 K – 175.5 K
   = 161.7 K = 161.7 °C

   Then find the molar mass (m) of methanol.

   m = 12.0 g + 4(1.0) g + 16.0 g
   = 32.0 g

   Then use the known values of m, ΔT, and the specific heat for methanol to calculate the heat absorbed.

   $q = m \times C \times \Delta T$
   $= 32.0 \text{ g} \times \dfrac{2.53 \text{ J}}{(\text{g} \cdot °\text{C})} \times 161.7 °\text{C}$
   = 13,091 J = 13.1 kJ

   Now you try it.

8. Calculate heat absorbed in region C for ammonia.
   Hint: What process is taking place in Region C?

   $\Delta H =$ _____

10. Calculate heat absorbed in each region for benzene (C_6H_6). [specific heat = 1.74 J/(g · °C)]
   Hint: You will need to do a calculation for region B.

   region A: $\Delta H =$ _____

   region B: $\Delta H =$ _____

   region C: $\Delta H =$ _____

Interpret Graphs Energy Changes in Reactions   Lesson 18.1

Preview the Graph

The graphs show the energy changes that occur during chemical reactions. The top graph shows how energy changes in an exothermic reaction. What type of reaction does the bottom graph show?

_____

_____

Look at the *x*-axis. The arrow pointing to the right shows that the reactions take place from left to right, with the reactants to the left and the products to the right.

Look at the *y*-axis. The variable is energy. What does the arrow pointing up represent?

_____

_____

In the top reaction, the reactants are hydrogen and oxygen molecules, and the product is water. In the bottom reaction, the reactant is water, and the products are hydrogen and oxygen molecules.

Both graphs have a peak in the middle of the graph.

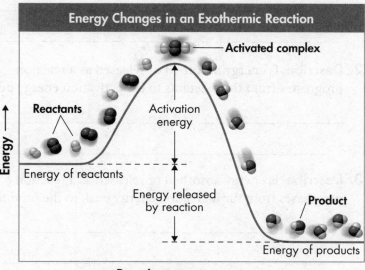

Energy Changes in an Exothermic Reaction

Activated complex

Reactants

Activation energy

Energy of reactants

Energy released by reaction

Product

Energy of products

Energy

Reaction progress ⟶

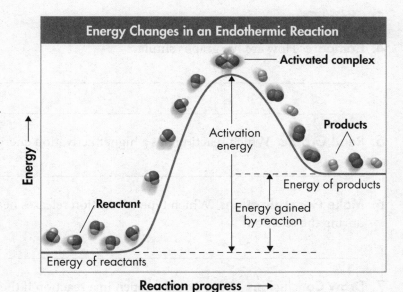

Energy Changes in an Endothermic Reaction

Activated complex

Activation energy

Products

Energy of products

Energy gained by reaction

Reactant

Energy of reactants

Energy

Reaction progress ⟶

The doubled-headed arrow beneath the peak shows the difference in energy between the reactants and the peak. This difference in energy is called the activation energy.

Analyze the Graph

Now you are ready to answer some more questions. As you read the questions:

▶ Highlight key words.
▶ Circle numbers and units.

Use the first question as an example.

1. **Read Graphs** On which graph is the energy of the products less than the energy of the reactants?

_____

_____

> **Try it!** Compare the energy of the reactants and the products on each graph.

2. **Describe** Is energy absorbed or released as a reaction progresses from the reactants to the activation energy peak?

_____

_____

> **Try it!** Compare the energy of the peak with the energy of the reactants on each graph.

3. **Describe** Is energy absorbed or released as a reaction progresses from the activation energy peak to the products?

_____

_____

> **Try it!** Compare the energy of the peak with the energy of the products on each graph.

On Your Own

4. **Compare** How are the graphs similar?

_____

_____

5. **Read Graphs** Which reaction has a higher activation energy?

_____

6. **Make Generalizations** Which type of reaction releases heat to the surroundings during the reaction?

_____

7. **Draw Conclusions** What would happen in a reaction if there were not enough energy available to cross the activation energy peak?

_____

_____

Interpret Graphs Catalysts and Activation Energy Lesson 18.1

Preview the Graph

Read the title of the graph. The graph shows the activation energy for an exothermic chemical reaction with a catalyst and for a chemical reaction without a catalyst.

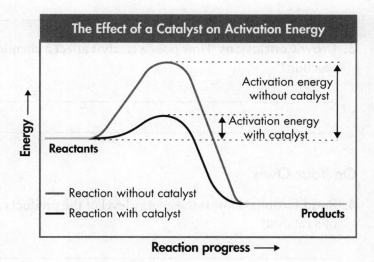

Look at the x-axis. The graph uses an arrow pointing to the right to show that the chemical reaction takes place from left to right across the graph, with the reactants to the left and the products to the right.

Look at the y-axis. What does the arrow above the y-axis label show?

_____

_____

Look at the key on the left side of the graph. The blue curve shows the activation energy for a reaction without a catalyst. What does the black curve show?

_____

Look at the double-headed arrows to the right of the peaks on the graph. What do these arrows indicate?

_____

Analyze the Graph

Now you are ready to answer some more questions. As you read the questions:

► Highlight key words.
► Circle numbers and units.

Use the first question as an example.

1. **Read Graphs** Look at the energy level of the reactants. How is it affected by the presence of a catalyst?

_____

_____

> **Try it!** Find the point on the y-axis that represents the energy of the reactants for each graph.

2. Read Graphs Which type of reaction, with a catalyst or without a catalyst, has a higher activation energy?

_____

_____

> **Try it!** Look at the color of the curve with the higher peak. Match the color to the key on the left side of the graph.

3. Draw Conclusions How does a catalyst affect a chemical reaction?

_____

_____

> **Try it!** Draw a line from each peak to the y-axis. Compare the energy values.

On Your Own

4. Read Graphs How is the energy level of the products affected by the presence of a catalyst?

_____

_____

5. Make Generalizations Does the catalyst change the amount of energy released in the reaction? Explain your answer.

_____

_____

_____

6. Apply Concepts How does using a catalyst change the amount of energy needed for a reaction to happen?

_____

_____

Interpret Graphs Rate Change During a Reaction   Lesson 18.2

Preview the Graph

Study the line graph. This graph shows how the concentration of a reactant changes over time. Time increases from left to right on the *x*-axis. The concentration of reactant A is shown on the *y*-axis. What does the arrow on the *y*-axis show?

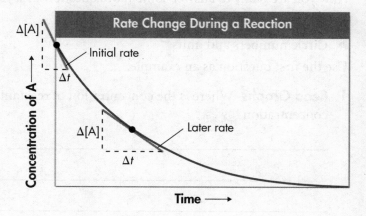

_____

_____

_____

The curved line shows how the concentration of A changes over time. There are two points that are shown on this line. Each point has a tangent line passing through it. Is a tangent line straight or curved?

_____

_____

Each tangent line forms a triangle with a vertical and a horizontal dashed line. These dashed lines allow you to find the slope, or change in rate, of the tangent line.

The symbols next to the dashed lines tell you what each line shows. Look at the symbols next to one of the vertical dashed lines. The symbol Δ represents change. The symbol [A] represents the concentration of reactant A. What does this vertical line show?

_____

_____

What does the horizontal dashed line above the Δt symbol show?

_____

_____

You can find the slope of each tangent line by dividing the change in the concentration of reactant A by the change in time. How could you use the slope of a tangent line to find the rate of the reaction?

_____

_____

_____

Analyze the Graph

Now you are ready to answer some more questions. As you read the questions:

▶ Highlight key words.

▶ Circle numbers and units.

Use the first question as an example.

1. Read Graphs Where is the concentration of reactant A highest? Where is the concentration lowest?

_____

_____

_____

> **Try it!** Find the point on the curve that is highest on the y-axis. Then find the point that is lowest on the y-axis.

2. Compare Which rate of reaction is greater: the initial rate or the later rate? *Hint:* The slope of the tangent line shows the rate of reaction.

_____

> **Try it!** Look for the tangent line that is closest to vertical. This would show a larger change in concentration over a shorter period of time.

On Your Own

3. Read Graphs How does the concentration of reactant A change over time?

_____

_____

4. Read graphs Where is the rate of reaction lowest? Explain how you know.

_____

_____

5. Apply Concepts Why does the concentration of reactant A change over time? *Hint:* Consider what happens as a chemical reaction takes place.

_____

_____

Interpret Graphs Multistep Reaction Curve

Lesson 18.2

Preview the Graph

Read the title of the graph. This graph shows the changes in energy that take place as reactants change to products during a chemical reaction. Look at the curved line on the graph. Each peak on the line represents a step during the reaction. How many steps does this reaction have?

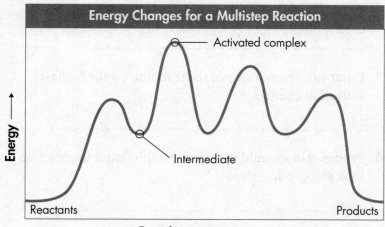

Energy Changes for a Multistep Reaction

Activated complex

Intermediate

Energy

Reactants

Products

Reaction progress ⟶

_____

Look at the *y*-axis. The arrow shows that energy increases from bottom to top along the axis. Look at the *x*-axis. What happens to the reaction as you move from left to right across the graph?

_____

_____

Look at the peaks and the valleys of the curve. Labels on the graph show what each peak or valley represents. Each peak represents an activated complex. What does each valley represent?

_____

_____

Analyze the Graph

Now you are ready to answer some more questions. As you read the questions:

▶ Highlight key words.
▶ Circle numbers and units.

Use the first question as an example.

1. **Read Graphs** How many activated complexes form before the final products of the reaction are formed?

_____

_____

Try it! Each peak in the curve shows the formation of an activated complex. Count the peaks to get your answer.

2. Read Graphs What are the products of the first three steps in the reaction?

_____

_____

> **Try it!** Each valley in the curve represents the product of a step in the reaction. Look at the label to see what these products are called.

3. Compare Which step of the reaction has the highest activation energy?

_____

> **Try it!** Find the peak that reaches the highest point on the y-axis.

4. Predict How would the curve be different if the reaction took place in five steps?

_____

_____

> **Try it!** Each peak represents a step during which an activated complex is formed. Each valley represents the formation of an intermediate.

On Your Own

5. Describe What happens to an intermediate when the step of the reaction that follows the intermediate takes place?

_____

_____

6. Read Graphs Describe what happens to energy during the entire reaction shown on the graph.

_____

_____

_____

_____

_____

7. Predict How many valleys would the curve have if the reaction took place in one step? Explain.

_____

_____

_____

Interpret Graphs Establishing Equilibrium

$$2SO_2(g) + O_2(g) \rightleftharpoons 2SO_3(g)$$

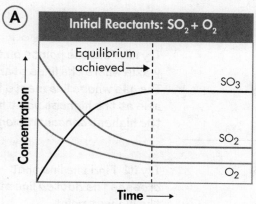

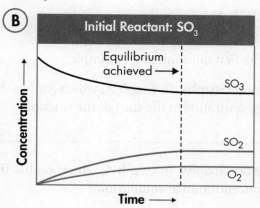

Preview the Graph

Look at the equation. The double arrow tells you that the reaction is reversible. It has a forward reaction and a reverse reaction. Sulfur dioxide (SO_2) and oxygen (O_2) are the reactants in the forward reaction. What is the reactant in the reverse reaction?

_____

Look at Graph A. It shows how the concentrations of SO_2, O_2, and SO_3 change over time when the reactants are SO_2 and O_2. Each gas has its own line. At the point where the axes meet, time is zero and concentration is zero. Which gas has a concentration of zero at the start of the reaction?

_____

Look at Graph B. It shows how the concentrations of SO_2, O_2, and SO_3 change over time when the reactant is SO_3. Which gases have a concentration of zero at the start of this reaction?

_____

Find the dotted vertical line on each graph. What point in the reaction does this line mark?

_____

_____

Analyze the Graph

Now you are ready to answer some more questions. As you read the questions:

► Highlight key words.
► Circle numbers and units.

Use the first question as an example.

1. **Read Graphs** In Graph A, which gas has the greatest concentration at the start of the reaction?

_____

> **Try it!** Find the points on the y-axis where the lines start. The gas whose line meets the axis at the highest point has the highest concentration.

2. **Read Graphs** In Graph A, which gas has the greatest concentration at equilibrium?

_____

> **Try it!** Find the line that crosses the dotted line at the highest point.

3. **Describe** In Graph A, what happens to the concentration of O_2 before equilibrium is achieved? What happens to its concentration after equilibrium is achieved?

_____

_____

> **Try it!** Observe the shape of the line for O_2 from the y-axis to the dotted line. Observe its shape after it crosses the dotted line.

On Your Own

4. **Describe** In Graph B, what happens to the concentration of O_2 between the start of the reaction and equilibrium? What happens to its concentration after equilibrium is achieved?

_____

_____

5. **Summarize** What happens to the concentrations of the reactants and products of a reversible reaction before equilibrium is achieved? What happens to their concentrations after equilibrium is achieved?

_____

_____

_____

More Practice Applying Le Châtelier's Principle   Lesson 18.3

Step-by-Step Practice

1. How is the equilibrium position of this reaction between gases in a closed container affected by the following changes?

$$PBr_5(g) + heat \rightleftharpoons PBr_3(g) + Br_2(g)$$

   a. Heat is added.
   b. Pressure is increased.
   c. PBr_5 is removed.

   ❶ Analyze Identify the relevant concepts.

According to Le Châtelier's principle, the equilibrium position will shift in the direction that relieves the stress on the system.

   ❷ Solve Apply the concepts to this problem.

   a. The stress is added heat. Removing heat will relieve the stress. Identify the reaction that removes heat from the system. In which direction will the equilibrium shift?

   The forward reaction removes heat from the system. The equilibrium shifts toward products.

   b. The stress is increased pressure. Decreasing the number of particles will decrease the pressure. Identify the reaction in which the number of particles is reduced. In which direction will the equilibrium shift?

   In the reverse reaction, two moles of particles produce one mole of particles. The equilibrium shifts toward reactants.

   c. The stress is removing PBr_5. PBr_5 is a reactant. Identify the reaction that lowers the concentration of a reactant. In which direction will the equilibrium shift?

   The forward reaction lowers the concentration of a reactant. The equilibrium shifts toward products.

....

2. The equation below describes a system in equilibrium. In which direction will the equilibrium shift if the following changes occur?

$$CaCO_3(s) \rightleftharpoons CaO(s) + CO_2(g) + heat$$

   a. CO_2 is removed.
   b. Heat is added.

   ❶ Analyze Identify the relevant concepts.

According to Le Châtelier's principle, the equilibrium position will shift in the direction that relieves the stress on the system.

2 Solve **Apply the concepts to this problem.**

a. CO_2 is a product. It needs to be replaced to relieve the stress on the system. Identify the reaction that produces more CO_2. In which direction must the equilibrium shift to relieve the stress?

The _____ reaction.

The shift is toward _____.

b. Heat has been added to the system. Identify the reaction that will remove heat. In which direction must the equilibrium shift to relieve the stress?

The _____ reaction.

The shift is toward _____.

On Your Own

3. Use Le Châtelier's principle to predict the effect each of the following changes will have on the equilibrium position for this reversible reaction.

$2NO(g) + Br_2(g) + heat \rightleftharpoons 2NOBr(g)$

a. The concentration of NO is increased.
b. Pressure is increased.
c. Heat is removed.

a. _____

b. _____

c. _____

4. What effect will each of the following changes have on the equilibrium position for this reversible reaction?

$3Fe(s) + 4H_2O(g) + heat \rightleftharpoons Fe_3O_4(s) + 4H_2(g)$

a. Fe_3O_4 is added.
b. Heat is added.

a. _____

b. _____

5. What effect will an increase in pressure have on the equilibrium position for this reversible reaction? Explain your answer. *Hint:* How many moles of gas are on each side of the equation?

$N_2(g) + O_2(g) \rightleftharpoons 2NO(g) + heat$

_____

_____

More Practice Finding Concentrations at Equilibrium Lesson 18.3

Step-by-Step Practice

1. The equilibrium constant for the decomposition of hydrogen bromide (HBr) is 4.75 at a certain temperature. The equilibrium mixture contains 3.04 mol H_2 and 1.0 mol Br_2. What is the equilibrium concentration of HBr?

$$2HBr(g) \rightleftharpoons H_2(g) + Br_2(g)$$

❶ **Analyze** **List the knowns and unknown.**

Knowns	Unknown
$[H_2]$(equilibrium) = 3.04 mol/L	$[HBr]$(equilibrium) = ? mol/L
$[Br_2]$(equilibrium) = 1.0 mol/L	
K_{eq} = 4.75	

❷ **Calculate** **Solve for the unknown.**

Use the balanced equation, equilibrium constant, and equilibrium constant expression to find the unknown concentration.

Write the equilibrium expression for the reaction.

$$K_{eq} = \frac{[H_2] \times [Br_2]}{[HBr]^2}$$

Rearrange the equation to solve for [HBr]. Multiply both sides of the expression by $[HBr]^2$. Divide both sides of the equation by K_{eq}.

$$[HBr]^2 = \frac{[H_2] \times [Br_2]}{K_{eq}}$$

Substitute the known values for K_{eq}, $[H_2]$, and $[Br_2]$ and solve.

$$[HBr]^2 = \frac{(3.04 \text{ mol/L}) \times (1.0 \text{ mol/L})}{4.75}$$

$$[HBr]^2 = 0.64 \text{ mol}^2/L^2$$

To find the concentration of $[H_2]$, take the square root of 0.64 mol²/L².

$$[HBr] = \sqrt{0.64 \text{ mol}^2/L^2} = 0.80 \text{ mol/L}$$

❸ **Evaluate** **Does the result make sense?**

With a value for K_{eq} of 4.75, it makes sense that the equilibrium mixture has significant amounts of reactant and products.

2. At a certain temperature, the K_{eq} for the decomposition of HCl is 1.3×10^3.

$$2HCl(g) \rightleftharpoons H_2(g) + Cl_2(g)$$

At equilibrium, 0.064 mol of HCl remain.
The concentration of Cl_2 is 2.58 mol/L.
What is the concentration of H_2?

① Analyze List the knowns and unknown.

Knowns	Unknown
[HCl](equilibrium) = 0.064 mol/L	[H$_2$](equilibrium) = ? mol/L
[Cl$_2$](equilibrium) = 2.58 mol/L	
K_{eq} = _____	

② Calculate Solve for the unknown.

Write the equilibrium expression for the reaction.

$$K_{eq} = \frac{[H_2] \times [Cl_2]}{}$$

Rearrange the equation to solve for the unknown.
Reverse the equation so the unknown is on the left.

$$[H_2] = \frac{K_{eq} \times}{[Cl_2]}$$

Substitute the known values for K_{eq}, [HCl], and [Cl$_2$]. The unit for concentration will be mol/L.

$$[H_2] = \frac{(1.3 \times 10^3) \times (\qquad)^2}{2.58 \text{ mol/L}}$$

$$= \underline{\qquad\qquad}$$

③ Evaluate Does the result make sense?

_____

_____

On Your Own

3. Carbon monoxide and hydrogen can combine to form methyl alcohol (CH$_3$OH).

$$CO(g) + 2H_2(g) \rightleftharpoons CH_3OH(g)$$

At equilibrium, the reaction contains 0.020 mol/L of CO and 0.60 mol/L H$_2$. The equilibrium constant is 2.2×10^2. What is the equilibrium concentration of CH$_3$OH?

18 Standardized Test Prep Tutor

Read the question. The highlighted words tell you what you will use to answer the question.

1. Which reaction is represented by the following expression for an equilibrium constant?

$$K_{eq} = \frac{[CO]^2 \times [O_2]}{[CO_2]^2}$$

(A) $2CO_2 \rightleftharpoons O_2 + 2CO$
(B) $CO_2^2 \rightleftharpoons O_2 + 2CO^2$
(C) $O_2 + 2CO \rightleftharpoons 2CO_2$
(D) $O_2 + CO_2 \rightleftharpoons CO_2^2$

❶ Analyze

Use the equilibrium constant expression to evaluate the answer choices.

❷ Solve

The concentrations of the products are shown in the numerator of the expression. Eliminate any answers that do not include O_2 and CO as products.

Answers C and D are not correct.

❸ Choose an Answer

Answer A and Answer B both have the correct reactant, which is CO_2. Find the correct answer by looking at the coefficient for CO_2 in the equations. The coefficient should match the exponent for CO_2 in the expression.

Answer A is correct.

Now you try it.

Which reaction is represented by the following expression for an equilibrium constant?

$$K_{eq} = \frac{[NH_3]^2}{[N_2] \times [H_2]^3}$$

(A) $2NH_3 \rightleftharpoons N_2 + 3H_2$
(B) $NH_3^2 \rightleftharpoons N_2 + 3H^2$
(C) $N_2 + 3H_2 \rightleftharpoons 2NH_3$
(D) $N_2 + H_2^3 \rightleftharpoons NH_3^2$

Use the table to answer Question 3.

ΔS	ΔH	ΔG	Spontaneous?
+	−	(a)	Yes
+	(b)	+ or −	At high *T*
(c)	+	+	No
−	−	(d)	At low *T*

2. The value of ΔG depends on the enthalpy (ΔH) and entropy (ΔS) terms for a reaction. The value of ΔG also varies as a function of temperature. Use the data in the table to identify the missing entries (a), (b), (c), and (d).

Address the missing entries one at a time. For all entries, refer to the equation for Gibbs free energy.

$$\Delta G = \Delta H - T\Delta S$$

Look at the first row in the table. The reaction is spontaneous. When a reaction is spontaneous, the value for ΔG is negative.

Entry (a) is negative (−).

Look at the second row. If ΔH were negative, the reaction would be spontaneous at all temperatures. But the reaction is spontaneous only at high temperatures. So ΔH must be positive.

Entry (b) is positive (+).

Look at the third row. If ΔS were positive, its value might be high enough to offset positive change in enthalpy. But the table says that the reaction is nonspontaneous. So ΔS must be negative.

Entry (c) is negative (−).

Look at the fourth row. The reaction is spontaneous only at low temperatures. So it must be nonspontaneous at high temperatures. The value for ΔG depends on the temperature.

Entry (d) is positive or negative (+ or −).

Now you try it.

Use the data in the table to identify the missing entries (a), (b), (c), and (d).

ΔH	ΔS	ΔG	Spontaneous?
+	(a)	+	No
(b)	−	+ or −	At low *T*
+	+	(c)	At high *T*
−	+	−	(d)

(a) = _____

(b) = _____

(c) = _____

(d) = _____

More Practice Calculating pH from [H⁺]

Step-by-Step Practice

1. A solution has a hydrogen-ion concentration of $2.2 \times 10^{-9}M$. What is the pH of the solution?

   ❶ **Analyze** List the known and the unknown.

Known	Unknown
$[H^+] = 2.2 \times 10^{-9}M$	pH = ?

   ❷ **Calculate** Solve for the unknown.

   Write the equation for finding pH from the hydrogen-ion concentration.

   $\quad pH = -\log[H^+]$

   Substitute the known $[H^+]$ into the equation. Use the log function on your calculator to find the pH.

   $\quad pH = -\log[2.2 \times 10^{-9}]$
   $\quad\quad = -(-8.65758) = 8.65758$
   $\quad pH = 8.66$

   ❸ **Evaluate** Does the result make sense?

   The hydrogen-ion concentration is between $1 \times 10^{-8}M$ and $1 \times 10^{-9}M$. So the pH should be between 8 and 9. The answer is rounded to two decimal places because the hydrogen-ion concentration has two significant figures.

   ....

2. Find the pH of a solution in which $[H^+] = 7.4 \times 10^{-2}M$.

   ❶ **Analyze** List the known and the unknown.

Known	Unknown
$[H^+] =$ _____	pH = ?

   ❷ **Calculate** Solve for the unknown.

   Write the equation for finding pH from the hydrogen-ion concentration.

   $\quad pH =$ _____

   Substitute the known $[H^+]$ into the equation. Use the log function on your calculator to find the pH.

   $\quad pH = -\log[$_____$]$
   $\quad pH =$ _____

   ❸ **Evaluate** Does the result make sense?

   The hydrogen-ion concentration is between $1 \times 10^{-1}M$ and $1 \times 10^{-2}M$. So the calculated pH should be between the values _____ and _____.

On Your Own

3. Find the pH of a solution with a hydrogen-ion concentration of $4.9 \times 10^{-11} M$.

4. Calculate the pH of a solution in which $[H^+] = 1.01 \times 10^{-1} M$.

5. The hydrogen-ion concentration of a solution is $0.0065 M$. What is the pH of the solution?

More Practice Calculating [H⁺] from pH

Lesson 19.2

Step-by-Step Practice

1. A solution of hydrochloric acid has a pH of 2.37. What is the hydrogen-ion concentration of this solution?

❶ Analyze List the known and the unknown.

Known	Unknown
pH = 2.37	[H⁺] = ? M

❷ Calculate Solve for the unknown.

Rearrange the equation for pH to isolate the unknown.

$$pH = -\log[H^+]$$
$$-\log[H^+] = pH$$
$$\log[H^+] = -pH$$
$$[H^+] = antilog(-pH)$$

Substitute the pH value into the equation and solve.

$$[H^+] = antilog(-2.37) = 4.265795 \times 10^{-3} M$$
$$[H^+] = 4.3 \times 10^{-3} M$$

❸ Evaluate Does the result make sense?

The pH is between 2 and 3, so the hydrogen-ion concentration should be between $1 \times 10^{-2} M$ and $1 \times 10^{-3} M$. The answer is rounded to two significant figures because the pH was measured to two decimal places.

....

2. What is the hydrogen-ion concentration of a solution with a pH of 12.7?

❶ Analyze List the known and the unknown.

Known	Unknown
pH = _____	[H⁺] = ? M

❷ Calculate Solve for the unknown.

Write the rearranged equation for pH with [H⁺] isolated on the left.

$$[H^+] = \underline{\hspace{3cm}}$$

Substitute the pH value into the equation and solve.

$$[H^+] = antilog(\underline{\hspace{2cm}})$$
$$[H^+] = \underline{\hspace{3cm}} M$$

③ Evaluate Does the result make sense?

The pH is between 12 and 13, so the calculated hydrogen-ion concentration should be between $1 \times$ _____ M and $1 \times$ _____ M.

On Your Own

3. Calculate $[H^+]$ for a solution that has a pH of 8.4.

4. Calculate the hydrogen-ion concentration for a solution with a pH of 5.75.

5. A solution has a pH of 0.855. What is the hydrogen-ion concentration of the solution?

Interpret Graphs Dissociation of Acids

Lesson 19.3

Preview the Graphs

Dissociation of an acid (HA) in water yields H_3O^+ and an anion, A^-. The bar graphs compare the degree of dissociation of a strong acid and a weak acid. The top graph models the dissociation of a strong acid. The bottom graph models the dissociation of a weak acid.

The variable on the y-axis of each graph is relative number of moles. The gray bar to the left of the arrow represents the amount of HA before dissociation. The bars to the right of the arrow represent the relative amounts of undissociated acid (HA), hydronium ion (H_3O^+), and anion (A^-) present in aqueous solution.

For a strong acid, does any HA remain undissociated in solution?

_____

For a weak acid, does any HA remain undissociated in solution?

_____

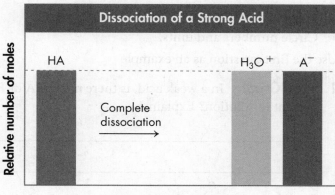

$$HA(aq) + H_2O(l) \longrightarrow H_3O^+(aq) + A^-(aq)$$

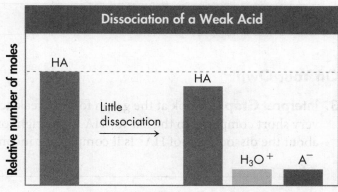

$$HA(aq) + H_2O(l) \rightleftharpoons H_3O^+(aq) + A^-(aq)$$

Look at the chemical equations under the graphs. Each equation describes the dissociation of an acid with the general formula HA. For a strong acid, the equation is written with a single arrow. What does a single arrow show?

_____

_____

For a weak acid, the dissociation equation is written with a double arrow. What does the double arrow show?

_____

_____

Analyze the Graph

Now you are ready to answer some more questions. As you read the questions:

▶ Highlight key words.

▶ Circle numbers and units.

Use the first question as an example.

1. Read Graphs In a weak acid, is there more HA or H_3O^+ present in solution? Explain.

_____

_____

> Try it! Look at the bottom graph. Compare the height of the bars for HA and H_3O^+ on the right side of the arrow.

2. Explain In the graph for the strong acid, why is there no bar representing HA to the right of the arrow?

_____

_____

> Try it! Look at the label above the arrow in the top graph.

On Your Own

3. Interpret Graphs Look at the graph for the weak acid. The bars for H_3O^+ and A^- are very short compared to the bar for HA to the right of the arrow. What does this tell you about the dissociation of HA? Is it complete or incomplete? Explain.

_____

_____

_____

4. Explain In the graph for the strong acid, why do the bars for H_3O^+ and A^- have the same height as the bar for HA? *Hint:* Look at the chemical equation under the graph.

_____

_____

5. Infer Consider the dissociation of a strong base with the general formula BOH.

$$BOH(aq) \longrightarrow B^+(aq) + OH^-(aq)$$

Would a graph that modeled this reaction more closely resemble the graph for the strong acid or the weak acid? Explain.

_____

_____

More Practice Determining Concentration by Titration Lesson 19.4

Step-by-Step Practice

1. Calculate the molarity of a nitric acid solution if 38 mL of the solution is neutralized by 16 mL of $0.25M$ $Ba(OH)_2$. The balanced equation for the reaction is:

$$2HNO_3(aq) + Ba(OH)_2(aq) \longrightarrow Ba(NO_3)_2(aq) + 2H_2O(l)$$

❶ **Analyze** List the knowns and the unknown.

Knowns	Unknown
$[Ba(OH)_2] = 0.25M$	$[HNO_3] = ? M$
$V_{Ba(OH)_2} = 0.016\,L$	
$V_{HNO_3} = 0.038\,L$	

❷ **Calculate** Solve for the unknown.

Use the molarity of the base as a conversion factor to convert the volume of base to moles of base.

$$0.016\text{ L Ba(OH)}_2 \times \frac{0.25\text{ mol Ba(OH)}_2}{1\text{ L Ba(OH)}_2}$$
$$= 0.0040\text{ mol Ba(OH)}_2$$

Use the mole ratio from the balanced equation to find the moles of acid.

$$0.0040\text{ mol Ba(OH)}_2 \times \frac{2\text{ mol HNO}_3}{1\text{ mol Ba(OH)}_2}$$
$$= 0.0080\text{ mol HNO}_3$$

Calculate the molarity by dividing moles of acid by liters of solution.

$$\text{molarity} = \frac{0.0080\text{ mol HNO}_3}{0.038\text{ L}}$$
$$= 0.21M\text{ HNO}_3$$

❸ **Evaluate** Does the result make sense?

If the acid had the same molarity as the base ($0.25M$), 19 mL of base would neutralize 38 mL of acid. Because the volume of base is less than 19 mL, the molarity of the acid must be less than $0.25M$.

....

2. What is the molarity of a solution of H_2SO_4 if 15.0 mL is neutralized by 75.0 mL of $0.200M$ KOH?

$$H_2SO_4(aq) + 2KOH(aq) \longrightarrow K_2SO_4(aq) + 2H_2O(l)$$

❶ **Analyze** List the knowns and the unknown.

Knowns	Unknown
$[KOH] = 0.200M$	$[H_2SO_4] = ? M$
$V_{KOH} = $ _____	
$V_{H_2SO_4} = $ _____	

❷ Calculate Solve for the unknown.

Use the molarity of the base as a conversion factor to convert the volume of base to moles of base.

$$_____ \text{ L KOH} \times \frac{_____}{1 \text{ L KOH}}$$

$$= _____$$

Use the mole ratio from the balanced equation to find the moles of acid.

$$_____ \text{ mol KOH} \times \frac{_____}{}$$

$$= _____ \text{ mol } H_2SO_4$$

Calculate the molarity by dividing moles of acid by liters of solution.

$$\text{molarity} = \frac{_____}{0.0150 \text{ L}}$$

$$= 0.500M \text{ } H_2SO_4$$

❸ Evaluate Does the result make sense?

If the acid had the same molarity as the base (0.200M), _____ mL of base would neutralize 15 mL of acid.

What volume of base was needed to neutralize the acid? _____ mL. Should the molarity of the acid be greater than or less than 0.200M? _____

On Your Own

3. What is the concentration of a solution of NaOH if 89.6 mL is neutralized by 56.0 mL of 0.400M HCl?

4. A solution of 0.150M H_3PO_4 is used to neutralize 38.0 mL of 0.200M Ba(OH)$_2$. How many milliliters of acid are required? The balanced equation for the neutralization reaction is:

$$2H_3PO_4(aq) + 3Ba(OH)_2(aq) \longrightarrow Ba_3(PO_4)_2(s) + 6H_2O(l)$$

Interpret Graphs Comparing Titration Curves

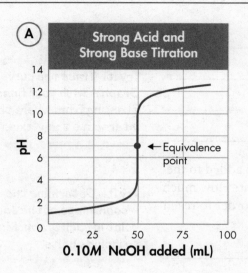

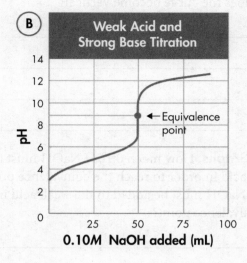

Preview the Graphs

Read the title of each graph. Graph A shows the titration curve for a strong acid and a strong base. Graph B shows the titration curve for a weak acid and a strong base.

In each graph, the variable on the *x*-axis is the volume of 0.10*M* NaOH added to the acid. What unit of measurement is used?

_____

The variable plotted on the *y*-axis is pH. The pH scale ranges from 0 to 14. A pH less than 7.0 indicates an acidic solution. What range of pH values indicates a basic solution?

_____

_____

Find the equivalence point on each graph. In an acid-base titration, the equivalence point is the point at which neutralization takes place. To the left of each equivalence point is a horizontal gray line. What does the line represent?

_____

_____

Analyze the Graphs

Now you are ready to answer some more questions. As you read the questions:

► Highlight key words.
► Circle numbers and units.

Use the first question as an example.

1. Describe Look at Graph A. Describe how the slope of the titration curve changes as base is added to the acid. At what point does the curve become vertical?

_____

_____

_____

_____

> **Try it!** Trace the curve of Graph A with your finger, starting from where the curve intersects the y-axis.

2. Read Graphs How much 0.10M NaOH must be added to the strong acid in order to reach the equivalence point? How much 0.10M NaOH must be added to the weak acid in order to reach the equivalence point?

_____

_____

> **Try it!** Determine the x-coordinate of the equivalence point in each graph. Make sure to include units.

3. Read Graphs What is the pH at the equivalence point for the strong acid-strong base titration? For the weak acid-strong base titration?

_____

_____

_____

> **Try it!** From the equivalence point on each graph, follow the gray horizontal line to where it intersects the y-axis.

On Your Own

4. Make Generalizations When an acid is titrated with a base, what happens to the pH of the solution as the titration nears the equivalence point?

_____

_____

5. Interpret Graphs At the equivalence point in Graph A, is the solution acidic, basic, or neutral? In Graph B? Explain.

_____

_____

_____

_____

6. Describe The weak acid used in the titration shown in Graph B is ethanoic acid ($CH_3COOH(aq)$). Write a balanced equation for the neutralization reaction between ethanoic acid and sodium hydroxide.

_____

19 Standardized Test Prep Tutor

Read the question. You need to figure out which combination of compound and ion would not be useful as a buffer.

8. Which combination of compound and ion would not make a useful buffer solution?
(A) ammonium ion and ammonia
(B) hydrogen carbonate ion and carbonic acid
(C) sulfate ion and sulfuric acid
(D) ethanoate ion and ethanoic acid

❶ Analyze

A buffer is a solution of a weak acid or a weak base and one of its salts. A weak acid or a weak base ionizes only slightly in an aqueous solution.

❷ Solve

Strong acids and strong bases ionize completely in an aqueous solution. Therefore, a strong acid or a strong base would not make a useful buffer solution. Which compound in the answer choices is a strong acid or a strong base?

_____ is a strong acid.

❸ Choose an Answer

Look at the answer choices. Which choice contains the strong acid that you identified? The correct answer is C.

Now you try it.

Which combination of compound and ion would not make a useful buffer solution?
(A) lactate ion and lactic acid
(B) dihydrogen phosphate ion and phosphoric acid
(C) hydroxide ion and potassium hydroxide
(D) hydrogen carbonate ion and carbonic acid

Which combination of compound and ion could be used to make a buffer solution?
(A) hydrogen ion and hydrochloric acid
(B) methanoate ion and methanoic acid
(C) nitrate ion and nitric acid
(D) hydroxide ion and sodium hydroxide

The lettered choices below refer to Questions 9–11. In each formula, P is the cation, and Q is the anion.

(A) PQ   (B) P_2Q_3 (C) PQ_3 (D) P_3Q

Which of the choices completes the general formula for the salt formed in each of the following neutralization reactions?

9. $H_3PO_4 + NaOH \longrightarrow$

10. $H_2SO_4 + Mg(OH)_2 \longrightarrow$

11. $HNO_3 + Al(OH)_3 \longrightarrow$

Answer choices A–D show possible general formulas for a salt formed during a neutralization reaction. For example, a salt with one cation and one anion would have the general formula PQ.

9. Which of the choices completes the general formula for the salt formed in the following neutralization reaction?

$H_3PO_4 + NaOH \longrightarrow$

In a neutralization reaction, an acid and a base react to produce a salt and water.

Complete the skeleton equation for the reaction.

The salt is $NaPO_4$. The sodium ion has a charge of 2^+, and the phosphate ion has a charge of 2^-. So the general formula contains one cation and one anion. Pick the answer choice that matches this general formula.

10. Which of the choices completes the general formula for the salt formed in the following neutralization reaction?

$H_2SO_4 + Mg(OH)_2 \longrightarrow$

Complete the skeleton equation for the reaction. Identify the general formula for the salt formed. Then choose the answer that matches that formula.

Now you try it.

In each formula, P is the cation, and Q is the anion.

(A) PQ   (B) P_2Q_3 (C) PQ_3 (D) P_3Q

11. Which of the choices completes the general formula for the salt formed in the following neutralization reaction?

$HNO_3 + Al(OH)_3 \longrightarrow$

$H_3PO_4 + NaOH \longrightarrow$

                 $NaPO_4 + H_2O$

General formula: PQ

The correct answer is A.

$H_2SO_4 + Mg(OH)_2 \longrightarrow$

_____ $+ H_2O$

General formula: _____

The correct answer is A.

skeleton equation:

_____ $+$ _____ $\longrightarrow$

_____ $+$ _____

More Practice Assigning Oxidation Numbers to Atoms   Lesson 20.2

Step-by-Step Practice

1. What is the oxidation number of each type of atom in bromic acid, $HBrO_3$?

> **❶ Analyze** **Identify the relevant concepts.**

Use the rules in lesson 20.2 of your textbook to assign or calculate oxidation numbers.

> **❷ Solve** **Apply the concepts to this problem.**

Use rules 2 and 3 to assign oxidation numbers to hydrogen and oxygen. According to rule 2, the oxidation number of hydrogen in a compound is +1. According to rule 3, the oxidation number of oxygen in a compound is −2.

$$\overset{+1\quad -2}{HBrO_3}$$

There are three oxygen atoms in the compound. Multiply the number of oxygen atoms by the oxidation number of oxygen to find the oxidation number for all three oxygen atoms. The oxidation number for the oxygen atoms is −6.

$$3 \times (-2) = -6$$

According to rule 5, the sum of the oxidation numbers of the atoms in a neutral compound must equal 0. Use this rule to find the oxidation number of bromine.

$$+1 + (+5) + (-6) = 0$$
$$\overset{+1\ +5\ -2}{HBrO_3}$$

....

2. What is the oxidation number of each type of atom in the chlorate ion, ClO_3^- ?

> **❶ Analyze** **Identify the relevant concepts.**

Use the rules in lesson 20.2 of your textbook to assign or calculate oxidation numbers.

> **❷ Solve** **Apply the concepts to this problem.**

Use rule 3 to find the oxidation number of oxygen in a compound. Then calculate the oxidation number for all three oxygen atoms.

$$\overset{-2}{ClO_3^-}$$

$$3 \times \underline{\quad\quad} = \underline{\quad\quad}$$

According to rule 6, the sum of the oxidation numbers must equal the ionic charge of a polyatomic ion. Use this information to find the oxidation number of chlorine.

$$\underline{\quad\quad} + \underline{\quad\quad} = -1$$

$$\underline{\quad\quad}$$

On Your Own

3. What is the oxidation number of each type of atom in sulfuric acid, H_2SO_4?

4. What is the oxidation number of each type of atom in the arsenate ion, AsO_4^{3-}?

5. What is the oxidation number of each type of atom in the compound potassium periodate, KIO_4? *Hint:* According to rule 1, the oxidation number of each ion is equal to its ionic charge.

More Practice

Balancing Redox Reactions by Oxidation-Number Change

Step-by-Step Practice

1. Use the oxidation-number-change method to balance this redox equation.

$$AsH_3(g) + NaClO_3(aq) \longrightarrow H_3AsO_4(aq) + NaCl(aq)$$

❶ **Analyze** Identify the relevant concepts.

Compare changes in the oxidation numbers for each atom in the equation. Then use coefficients to make the total increase in oxidation number equal to the total decrease in oxidation number in the redox equation.

❷ **Solve** Apply the concepts to this situation.

Step 1: Start with the unbalanced skeleton equation for the redox reaction. Assign an oxidation number to each of the atoms in the equation. Write the numbers above the atoms.

$$\overset{-3\ +1}{AsH_3}(g) + \overset{+1\ +5\ -2}{NaClO_3}(aq) \longrightarrow \overset{+1\ +5\ -2}{H_3AsO_4}(aq) + \overset{+1\ -1}{NaCl}(aq)$$

Step 2: Identify the atoms that are oxidized and the atoms that are reduced.

Arsenic's oxidation number increases from −3 to +5, so arsenic is oxidized. Chlorine's oxidation number decreases from +5 to −1, so chlorine is reduced.

Step 3: Use one line to connect the atoms that are oxidized. Use another line to connect the atoms that are reduced. Write the change in oxidation number at the midpoint of each line.

+8 (oxidation)

$$\overset{-3\ +1}{AsH_3}(g) + \overset{+1\ +5\ -2}{NaClO_3}(aq) \longrightarrow \overset{+1\ +5\ -2}{H_3AsO_4}(aq) + \overset{+1\ -1}{NaCl}(aq)$$

−6 (reduction)

Step 4: Figure out which coefficients will make the total increase in oxidation number equal to the total decrease in oxidation number. In this equation, three arsenic atoms are oxidized for every four chlorine atoms that are reduced. Put the coefficient 3 in front of AsH_3 and H_3AsO_4. Put the coefficient 4 in front of $NaClO_3$ and NaCl.

$3 \times (+8) = +24$

$$\overset{-3\ +1}{AsH_3}(g) + \overset{+1\ +5\ -2}{NaClO_3}(aq) \longrightarrow \overset{+1\ +5\ -2}{H_3AsO_4}(aq) + \overset{+1\ -1}{NaCl}(aq)$$

$4 \times (-6) = -24$

$$3AsH_3(g) + 4NaClO_3(aq) \longrightarrow$$
$$3H_3AsO_4(aq) + 4NaCl(aq)$$

Step 5: Make sure the equation is balanced for both atoms and charge. This equation is balanced, so no more changes are needed.

2. Chromium will reduce the tin(IV) ion in the following reaction:

$$Cr(s) + SnBr_4(aq) \longrightarrow CrBr_3(aq) + SnBr_2(aq)$$

Use the oxidation-number-change method to balance the redox equation.

❶ Analyze Identify the relevant concepts.

Compare changes in the oxidation numbers for each atom in the equation. Then use coefficients to make the total increase in oxidation number equal to the total decrease in oxidation number in the redox equation.

❷ Solve Apply the concepts to this situation.

Step 1: Start with an unbalanced skeleton equation for the redox reaction. Assign an oxidation number to each of the atoms in the equation.

$$\overset{0}{Cr}(s) + \overset{+4}{Sn}\overset{-1}{Br_4}(aq) \longrightarrow \overset{+3}{Cr}\overset{-1}{Br_3}(aq) + \overset{+2}{Sn}\overset{-1}{Br_2}(aq)$$

Write the numbers above the atoms.

Step 2: Identify the atoms that are oxidized and the atoms that are reduced.

Chromium's oxidation number increases, so chromium is _____.

Tin's oxidation number decreases, so tin is _____.

Step 3: Use one line to connect the atoms that are oxidized. Use another line to connect the atoms that are reduced.

$$\overset{+3}{\overbrace{\overset{0}{Cr}(s) + \overset{+4}{Sn}\overset{-1}{Br_4}(aq) \longrightarrow \overset{+3}{Cr}\overset{-1}{Br_3}(aq) + \underset{-2}{\underbrace{\overset{+2}{Sn}\overset{-1}{Br_2}}}(aq)}}$$

Write the change in oxidation number at the midpoint of each line.

Step 4: Use coefficients to make the total increase in oxidation number equal to the total decrease in oxidation number.

$$\overset{2\times(+3)\,=\,+6}{\overbrace{\overset{0}{Cr}(s) + \overset{+4}{Sn}\overset{-1}{Br_4}(aq) \longrightarrow \overset{+3}{Cr}\overset{-1}{Br_3}(aq) + \underset{3\times(-2)\,=\,-6}{\underbrace{\overset{+2}{Sn}\overset{-1}{Br_2}}}(aq)}}$$

$$\_\_Cr(s) + \_\_SnBr_4(aq) \longrightarrow$$
$$\_\_CrBr_3(aq) + \_\_SnBr_2(aq)$$

Step 5: Is the equation balanced for both atoms and charge? _____.

On Your Own

3. Use the steps of the oxidation-number-change method to balance this redox equation.

$$SO_2(g) + HNO_2(aq) \longrightarrow H_2SO_4(aq) + NO(g)$$

a. Assign an oxidation number to each of the atoms in the equation.

b. Use lines to connect the atoms that are oxidized and the atoms that are reduced. Write the change in each oxidation number at the midpoint of each line.

c. Use coefficients to make the total increase in oxidation number equal to the total decrease in oxidation number.

d. Write the balanced redox equation.

4. Use the oxidation-number-change method to balance this redox equation.

$$Al(s) + MnO_2(s) \longrightarrow Al_2O_3(s) + Mn(s)$$

20 Standardized Test Prep Tutor

Read the question. Three of the processes are oxidations. You need to find the one that is *not* an oxidation.

1. Which of these processes is not an oxidation?
   (A) a decrease in oxidation number
   (B) a complete loss of electrons
   (C) a gain of oxygen
   (D) a loss of hydrogen by a covalent molecule

❶ Analyze

Describe what could happen to a substance during oxidation. Then compare your descriptions to the answer choices.

❷ Solve

Are electrons gained or lost during oxidation?

Is oxygen gained or lost during oxidation?

Is hydrogen gained or lost during oxidation of a covalent compound?

What happens to the oxidation number of a substance when it is oxidized?

Electrons are _____ lost during oxidation.

Oxygen is _____ during oxidation.

Hydrogen is _____ during oxidation of a covalent compound.

The oxidation number of a substance _____ when it is oxidized.

❸ Choose an Answer

Look at the answer choices. Choices B, C, and D are examples of oxidation. The correct answer is A.

Now you try it.

Which of these processes is not a reduction?
(A) a partial gain of electrons
(B) a shift of electrons away from an atom in a covalent bond
(C) a loss of oxygen
(D) a decrease in oxidation number

Use the table to answer Questions 7–9.

Metal		Metal ion	
	K	K⁺	
3	Ca	Ca²⁺	
	Na	Na⁺	
	Mg	Mg²⁺	
4	Fe	Fe²⁺	
	Sn	Sn²⁺	
	Pb	Pb²⁺	
5	Cu	Cu²⁺	
	Ag	Ag⁺	

Table showing Metal column (K, Ca, Na, Mg, Fe, Sn, Pb, Cu, Ag) grouped 3, 4, 5 with Arrow 1 pointing up labeled 1, and Metal ion column (K^+, Ca^{2+}, Na^+, Mg^{2+}, Fe^{2+}, Sn^{2+}, Pb^{2+}, Cu^{2+}, Ag^+) with Arrow 2 pointing down labeled 2.

7. Which arrow indicates increasing ease of oxidation? Of reduction?

8. Which numbered group of metals are the strongest reducing agents? Which numbered group of metals are the most difficult to oxidize?

9. Which is a stronger oxidizing agent, Na or Fe?

Focus on one question at a time.

7. Which arrow indicates increasing ease of oxidation? Of reduction?

Metals in Groups 1 and 2 lose electrons more easily than other metals. Metals at the top of Arrow 1 in the diagram are in Groups 1 and 2. So the metals at the top of each list lose electrons most easily. The metals at the bottom of each list gain electrons most easily.

Arrow 1 shows increasing ease of _____.

Arrow 2 shows increasing ease of _____.

8. Which numbered group of metals are the strongest reducing agents? Which numbered group of metals are the most difficult to oxidize?

The chemical species that is oxidized is the reducing agent. You know from Question 7 that the metals at the top of the list are the easiest to oxidize. The metals at the bottom would be the hardest to oxidize.

The strongest reducing agents are the metals in _____.

The metals that are the most difficult to oxidize are in _____.

Now you try it.

9. Which is a stronger oxidizing agent, Na or Fe?

_____

_____

Interpret Data Activity Series of Metals

Preview the Table

The table has three columns. Look at the column on the left. Find the arrow pointing down with the label "decreasing activity." The activity being described is oxidation.

Read the labels above and below the arrow. In the table, where are metals that are most easily oxidized found? Where are metals that are least easily oxidized found?

_____

_____

_____

_____

	Activity Series of Metals	
	Element	**Oxidation half-reaction**
Most active and most easily oxidized	Lithium	$Li(s) \longrightarrow Li^+(aq) + e^-$
	Potassium	$K(s) \longrightarrow K^+(aq) + e^-$
	Barium	$Ba(s) \longrightarrow Ba^{2+}(aq) + 2e^-$
	Calcium	$Ca(s) \longrightarrow Ca^{2+}(aq) + 2e^-$
	Sodium	$Na(s) \longrightarrow Na^+(aq) + e^-$
Decreasing activity	Magnesium	$Mg(s) \longrightarrow Mg^{2+}(aq) + 2e^-$
	Aluminum	$Al(s) \longrightarrow Al^{3+}(aq) + 3e^-$
	Zinc	$Zn(s) \longrightarrow Zn^{2+}(aq) + 2e^-$
	Iron	$Fe(s) \longrightarrow Fe^{2+}(aq) + 2e^-$
	Nickel	$Ni(s) \longrightarrow Ni^{2+}(aq) + 2e^-$
	Tin	$Sn(s) \longrightarrow Sn^{2+}(aq) + 2e^-$
	Lead	$Pb(s) \longrightarrow Pb^{2+}(aq) + 2e^-$
	Copper	$Cu(s) \longrightarrow Cu^{2+}(aq) + 2e^-$
	Silver	$Ag(s) \longrightarrow Ag^+(aq) + e^-$
Least active and least easily oxidized	Mercury	$Hg(s) \longrightarrow Hg^{2+}(aq) + 2e^-$
	Gold	$Au(s) \longrightarrow Au^{3+}(aq) + 3e^-$

The middle column lists selected elements. The column on the right lists a half-reaction for each element. A half-reaction shows either an oxidation or a reduction. Which kind of half-reactions are shown in the table?

_____

The numeral 1 is usually omitted in the symbol for an ion. Look at the half-reactions. Find the ions that have a 1+ charge.

_____

Analyze the Data

Now you are ready to answer some more questions. As you read the questions:

▶ Highlight key words.
▶ Circle numbers and units.

Use the first question as an example.

1. Read Tables When nickel is oxidized, what is the charge on the ion that forms? How many electrons are lost?

_____

_____

> **Try it!** Find the half-reaction for nickel. Identify the charge and the number of electrons.
> $Ni(s) \longrightarrow Ni^{2+}(aq) + 2e^-$

2. Compare Which metal is more easily oxidized, lead or magnesium?

_____

_____

> **Try it!** Magnesium is above lead in the table. More active metals are higher in the table.

3. Predict A strip of copper is placed in a solution of silver nitrate. A redox reaction occurs. What will happen to the copper atoms? What will happen to the silver ions?

_____

_____

> **Try it!** Both oxidation and reduction happen during a redox reduction. The more active metal is oxidized. The less active metal is reduced.

On Your Own

4. Read Tables When potassium is oxidized, what is the charge on the ion that forms? How many electrons are lost? *Hint:* Often the coefficient 1 is not included in equations.

_____

_____

5. Compare Which metal is more easily oxidized, calcium or zinc? Explain.

_____

_____

6. Predict Will a reaction occur when a strip of copper is placed in a solution of magnesium chloride? Explain your answer.

_____

_____

More Practice Calculating the Standard Cell Potential   Lesson 21.2

Step-by-Step Practice

1. Find the cell reaction for a voltaic cell constructed from the following half-cell reactions. Then, calculate the standard cell potential for the cell.

$$Ag^+ + e^- \longrightarrow Ag \quad E^0_{Ag^+} = +0.80 \text{ V}$$

$$Cl_2 + 2e^- \longrightarrow 2Cl^- \quad E^0_{Cl^-} = +1.36 \text{ V}$$

❶ **Analyze** List the knowns and the unknowns.

Knowns	Unknowns
$E^0_{Ag^+} = +0.80 \text{ V}$	cell reaction = ?
$E^0_{Cl^-} = +1.36 \text{ V}$	$E^0_{cell} = ? \text{ V}$

❷ **Calculate** Solve for the unknown.

The half-cell reaction for chlorine has a more positive reduction potential, so it will be the reduction reaction. Reverse the order of the silver reaction to show it as an oxidation.

Oxidation: $Ag(s) \longrightarrow Ag^+(aq) + e^-$
Reduction: $Cl_2(g) + 2e^- \longrightarrow 2Cl^-(aq)$

Check if the number of electrons lost in the oxidation reaction is the same as the number of electrons gained in the reduction.

Silver loses 1 electron.
Chlorine gains 2 electrons.

Multiply the silver reaction by the factor needed so that the electrons will cancel when the half-reactions are added.

$$2Ag(s) \longrightarrow 2Ag^+(aq) + 2e^-$$
$$Cl_2(g) + 2e^- \longrightarrow 2Cl^-(aq)$$
$$\overline{2Ag(s) + Cl_2(g) \longrightarrow 2Ag^+(aq) + 2Cl^-(aq)}$$

Write the equation for standard cell potential.

$$E^0_{cell} = E^0_{red} - E^0_{oxid}$$

Substitute reduction potential values for chlorine and silver.

$$E^0_{cell} = E^0_{Cl^-} - E^0_{Ag^+}$$
$$E^0_{cell} = +1.36 \text{ V} - (+0.80 \text{ V}) = +0.56 \text{ V}$$

❸ **Evaluate** Does the result make sense?

The reduction potentials of the reduction and the oxidation are both positive but the reduction potential of the oxidation is smaller. The result is a positive cell potential.

2. Determine the overall cell reaction and standard cell potential for a voltaic cell made from the following half-cells.

$$Cd(s) \longrightarrow Cd^{2+}(aq) + 2e^- \quad E^0_{Cd^{2+}} = -0.40 \text{ V}$$

$$Hg_2^{2+}(aq) + 2e^- \longrightarrow 2Hg(s) \quad E^0_{Hg_2^{2+}} = +0.79 \text{ V}$$

❶ Analyze List the knowns and the unknowns.

Knowns	Unknowns
$E^0_{Cd^{2+}} =$ _____	cell reaction = ?
$E^0_{Hg_2^{2+}} =$ _____	$E^0_{cell} =$

❷ Calculate Solve for the unknown.

Identify the reaction with the more positive reduction potential and label it as the reduction reaction. Reverse the order of the oxidation reaction.

Oxidation: _____ $\longrightarrow$ _____

Reduction: _____ $\longrightarrow$ _____

_____

Cell reaction: _____

Check to make sure that the electrons will cancel when the half-reactions are added.

Use the equation for standard cell potential, substitute reduction potential values, and solve.

$$E^0_{cell} = \text{_____} - \text{_____}$$

$$E^0_{cell} = \text{_____} - \text{_____} = \text{_____}$$

❸ Evaluate Does the result make sense?

The reduction potential of the reduction is _____ and the reduction potential of the oxidation is _____ . The result is a _____ cell potential.

On Your Own

3. Find the overall cell reaction and the standard cell potential for a cell composed of the following half reactions.

$$Fe^{3+}(aq) + e^- \longrightarrow Fe^{2+}(aq) \quad E^0_{Fe^{3+}} = +0.77 \text{ V}$$

$$Sn^{2+}(aq) + 2e^- \longrightarrow Sn(s) \quad E^0_{Sn^{2+}} = -0.14 \text{ V}$$

21 Standardized Test Prep Tutor

Read the question. You need to figure out the type of half-reaction and the electrode where it happens.

4. Magnesium metal is prepared by the electrolysis of molten $MgCl_2$. One half-reaction is:

$$Mg^{2+}(l) + 2e^- \longrightarrow Mg(l)$$

Which of the following statements is true?
(A) This half-reaction occurs at the cathode.
(B) Magnesium ions are oxidized.
(C) Chloride ions are reduced at the anode.
(D) Chloride ions gain electrons during this process.

❶ Analyze

In the half-reaction, Mg^{2+} gains electrons. The magnesium half-reaction is a reduction.

❷ Solve

Look at answer A. You cannot rule it out because it does not mention reduction.

Look at answer B. It says that magnesium ions are oxidized.   Answer B is incorrect.

Look at answer C. It says that chloride ions are reduced. You   Answer C is incorrect.
know that magnesium ions are reduced.

Look at answer D. It says that chloride ions gain electrons.   Answer D is incorrect.
You know that magnesium ions gain electrons.

❸ Choose an Answer

The only answer that has not been eliminated is A. So answer A is correct.

Now you try it.

Lithium metal is prepared by the electrolysis of molten LiBr. One half-reaction is:

$$2Br^-(l) \longrightarrow Br_2(l) + 2e^-$$

Which of the following statements is true?
(A) This half-reaction occurs at the cathode.
(B) Lithium ions are oxidized.
(C) Bromide ions are reduced at the anode.
(D) Lithium ions gain electrons during this process.

Use the data table to answer Questions 6, 10, and 12. Hydrogen is included as a reference point for the metals.

Activity Series of Selected Metals	
Element	**Oxidation half-reaction**
Lithium	$Li(s) \longrightarrow Li^+(aq) + e^-$
Potassium	$K(s) \longrightarrow K^+(aq) + e^-$
Sodium	$Na(s) \longrightarrow Na^+(aq) + e^-$
Aluminum	$Al(s) \longrightarrow Al^{3+}(aq) + 3e^-$
Zinc	$Zn(s) \longrightarrow Zn^{2+}(aq) + 2e^-$
Iron	$Fe(s) \longrightarrow Fe^{2+}(aq) + 2e^-$
Hydrogen	$H_2(g) \longrightarrow 2H^+(aq) + 2e^-$
Copper	$Cu(s) \longrightarrow Cu^{2+}(aq) + 2e^-$

Focus on one question at a time.

6. Which metal will more easily lose an electron: sodium or potassium?

   In the activity series, the elements that are more likely to lose electrons are at the top. Potassium is listed above sodium. So, potassium is more likely to lose an electron.

   Potassium loses an electron more easily than sodium.

10. Would a copper strip placed in a solution containing zinc ions react spontaneously with the zinc ions? Explain your reasoning.

    Zinc is above copper in the activity series, which means that zinc is more likely to lose electrons than copper is.

    The reaction would not be spontaneous because copper would have to lose electrons to react with zinc and it is less likely to do that than zinc is.

12. Write the half-reaction for the reduction of aluminum ions.

    The table gives the oxidation half-reaction for aluminum. The reduction half-reaction goes in the opposite direction, showing a gain of electrons instead of a loss.

    $Al^{3+}(aq) + 3e^- \longrightarrow Al(s)$

Interpret Graphs Properties of Straight-Chain Alkanes   Lesson 22.1

Preview the Graph

This graph shows two properties of straight-chain alkanes: melting point and boiling point. These properties vary with the number of carbons in the molecule.

Find the dots on the graph that show the melting point. These dots are gray. Find the dots that show the boiling point. What color are the boiling point dots?

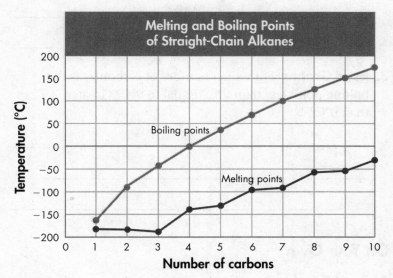

Melting and Boiling Points of Straight-Chain Alkanes

_____

Number of carbons is the variable on the *x*-axis.
What happens to the number of carbons as you move from left to right across the graph?

_____

_____

Melting and boiling points are given for straight-chain alkanes that have a wide range of carbon atoms. The minimum number of carbons is 1. What is the maximum number of carbons?

_____

_____

Temperature, in °C, is the variable on the *y*-axis. What is the range of temperature values shown on the graph?

_____

_____

Analyze the Graph

Now you are ready to answer some more questions. As you read the questions:

▶ Highlight key words.
▶ Circle numbers and units.

Use the first question as an example.

1. **Read Graphs** What is the boiling point of a straight-chain alkane with (1 carbon)?

_____

> **Try it!** Find 1 on the x-axis. Draw a vertical line to the blue point directly above the 1. Then draw a horizontal line to the y-axis. Estimate the temperature value.

2. Compare As you move from left to right across the graph, do the boiling points increase or decrease?

_____

_____

> **Try it!** Compare the y-axis values of the boiling points as you trace the line from left to right.

3. Read Graphs For which number of carbon(s) is the boiling point less than 0°C? Equal to 0°C? Greater than 0°C?

_____

_____

_____

> **Try it!** Find the blue point that has a y-value of 0°C. Draw a vertical line to the x-axis. The points to the left of the line have boiling points below 0°C. The points to the right of the line have boiling points greater than 0°C.

On Your Own

4. Read Graphs Describe the melting point graph as you move from left to right across the graph.

_____

5. Read Graphs For which number of carbon(s) is the melting point less than 0°C? Equal to 0°C? Greater than 0°C?

_____

_____

6. Compare How do the melting point and boiling point compare for each number of carbons?

_____

7. Make Generalizations What affect does increasing the number of carbons have on the melting point and boiling points?

_____

_____

8. Predict Use the patterns in the graphs to estimate a boiling point and a melting point for a straight-chain alkane with 11 carbons.

_____

More Practice
Drawing Formulas for Branched-Chain Alkanes

Lesson 22.1

Step-by-Step Practice

1. Draw the structural formula for 2,4-dimethylhexane.

> **❶ Analyze** Identify the relevant concepts.

The part of the name that ends in -*ane* is the parent hydrocarbon. The numbers and words in the prefix indicate the types of substituents, the number of times each appears, and their locations on the parent chain. Add hydrogens as needed to complete the structural formula.

> **❷ Solve** Apply concepts to this situation.

Identify the parent hydrocarbon and the prefix for 2, 4-dimethylhexane.

The parent hydrocarbon is hexane.

The prefix is 2,4-dimethyl-.

Draw a chain of carbons for the parent hydrocarbon and number the carbon atoms. Hexane has six carbon atoms.

$$C—C—C—C—C—C$$
$$1 \to 2 \to 3 \to 4 \to 5 \to 6$$

Identify the number and type of substituents. The prefix tells you that the substituents are two methyl groups.

Attach the methyl groups to the carbons numbered 2 and 4.

Complete the structure by adding hydrogens so that each carbon has four bonds.

- -

2. Draw the structure for the branched-chain hydrocarbon 3-ethyl-2-methylpentane.

> **❶ Analyze** Identify the relevant concepts.

Identify the parent hydrocarbon. Identify the substituents and their locations on the parent chain. Add hydrogens as needed to complete the structural formula.

> **❷ Solve** Apply concepts to this situation.

Identify the parent hydrocarbon and the prefix.

The parent hydrocarbon is pentane.

The prefix is _____.

Draw the carbons in the parent chain. Number the carbon atoms. Pentane has five carbon atoms.

C — C — C — C — C

Identify the number and type of substituents.

There is ____ ethyl group and ____ methyl group.

Attach the substituents to the carbons identified in the prefix. Complete the structure by adding hydrogens so that each carbon has four bonds.

C — C — C — C — C

On Your Own

3. Draw the structural formula for the branched hydrocarbon 2,3,4-trimethylhexane.

4. The hydrocarbon 2,2,3-trimethylbutane is sometimes used as an additive in fuel for airplanes. Draw the structural formula for this hydrocarbon.

5. Draw the structural formula of 3-ethyl-4-methylhexane.

22 Standardized Test Prep Tutor

Read the question.

1. What is the name of the compound with the following structural formula?

$$CH_3 - \underset{\underset{H}{|}}{\overset{\overset{CH_3}{|}}{C}} - \underset{\underset{H}{|}}{\overset{\overset{H}{|}}{C}} - \underset{\underset{H}{|}}{\overset{\overset{CH_3}{|}}{C}} - CH_3$$

(A) 1,2,3,3-tetramethylpropane   (C) 2,4-dimethylpentane
(B) heptane   (D) 1,5-dimethylbutane

❶ Analyze

There are five carbon atoms in the main chain. What is the name of the parent carbon?

The parent carbon is pentane.

Number the carbons in the main chain to give substituent groups the smallest numbers possible. Identify the substituent groups and their positions.

$${}^1CH_3 - \overset{2}{\underset{\underset{H}{|}}{\overset{\overset{CH_3}{|}}{C}}} - \overset{3}{\underset{\underset{H}{|}}{\overset{\overset{H}{|}}{C}}} - \overset{4}{\underset{\underset{H}{|}}{\overset{\overset{CH_3}{|}}{C}}} - {}^5CH_3$$

Substituent groups: 2-methyl, 4-methyl

❷ Solve

Combine all the parts of the name. Use the correct prefix to show that the compound has two methyl groups.

2,4-dimethylpentane

❸ Choose an Answer

Look at the answer choices. Find the choice that matches the name of the compound. The correct answer is C.

Now you try it.

What is the name of the compound with the following structural formula?

$$CH_3 - \underset{\underset{CH_3}{|}}{\overset{\overset{CH_3}{|}}{C}} - CH_2 - \underset{\overset{|}{CH_3}}{\overset{}{CH}} - CH_3$$

(A) 2,2,4-trimethylpentane   (C) 2,4,4-trimethylpentane
(B) 1,1,1,3-tetramethylbutane   (D) octane

Read the question. The highlighted word tells you the kind of isomer you are looking for.

5. A constitutional isomer of heptane is:
   (A) methylbenzene.
   (B) 3,3-dimethylpentane.
   (C) cycloheptane.
   (D) 3-methylhexene.

❶ Analyze

All constitutional isomers of heptane have the formula C_7H_{16}. Each compound listed in the answer choices has seven carbon atoms. Find the compound that also has 16 hydrogen atoms.

❷ Solve

Look at the answer choices.

Answer choice A describes a methyl group attached to a benzene ring. Draw the structural formula.

Use the structure to find the molecular formula of methylbenzene.

Methylbenzene: _____

Answer choice B describes two methyl groups attached to a pentane chain. Draw the structural formula.

Find the molecular formula.

3,3-dimethylpentane: _____

❸ Choose an Answer

3,3-dimethylpentane has 16 hydrogen atoms. So the correct answer is B.

Now you try it.

A constitutional isomer of octane is:
(A) cyclooctane.
(B) 2,4-dimethylhexene.
(C) 3-ethyl-2-methylpentene.
(D) 2,2,3,3-tetramethylbutane.

Interpret Data

Some Organic Compounds with Three Carbons

Lesson 23.3

Some Organic Compounds with Three Carbons			
Compound	Structural formula	Boiling point (°C)	Primary intermolecular interactions
Propane	$CH_3—CH_2—CH_3$	−42	Dispersion forces
Propanal	$CH_3—CH_2—\overset{\overset{O}{\|\|}}{C}—H$	49	Polar-polar interactions
Propanone	$CH_3—\overset{\overset{O}{\|\|}}{C}—CH_3$	56	Polar-polar interactions
1-propanol	$CH_3—CH_2—CH_2—O—H$	97	Hydrogen bonding

Preview the Table

The table compares four organic compounds that have the same number of carbon atoms. The first column lists the names of the four compounds. What is similar about the names of the compounds?

_____

Look at the second column, which shows the structural formula for each compound. What is similar about the structural formulas of the compounds? What is different?

_____

_____

_____

The third column shows the boiling point for each compound. What units are used for boiling point?

_____

Analyze the Table

Now you are ready to answer some more questions. As you read the questions:

▶ Highlight key words.
▶ Circle numbers and units.

Use the first question as an example.

1. **Read Tables** Which compound in the table has the lowest boiling point? Which compound has the highest boiling point? List these boiling points.

_____

_____

> **Try it!** Look at the boiling point column. Find the lowest and highest values. Move your finger to the left across each row to find the compounds with those values.

2. **Identify** Which two compounds have the same primary intermolecular interactions? What are those interactions?

_____

_____

> **Try it!** Look at the column showing primary intermolecular interactions. Find two interactions that are the same. Write down the names of those compounds.

3. **Compare** How is the structural formula for propanal different from the structural formula for 1-propanol?

_____

_____

_____

> **Try it!** Count the different types of atoms shown for each compound. Look at which atoms are joined together with lines that represent bonds. Look for double lines, which show a double bond.

On Your Own

4. **Identify** A ketone has a carbon atom that is double-bonded to oxygen to form a carbonyl group. That carbon is also bonded to two other carbon atoms. Which compound in the table is a ketone?

_____

5. **Compare** How do the boiling points of the two compounds you identified in Question 2 compare to the other two boiling points listed in the table?

_____

_____

_____

6. **Make Generalizations** What is the apparent relationship between intermolecular interactions and the boiling point of organic compounds?

_____

_____

_____

23 Standardized Test Prep Tutor

The lettered choices below refer to Questions 4–7. A lettered choice may be used once, more than once, or not at all.

    (A) alcohol   **(C)** carboxylic acid

    (B) ketone   **(D)** ether

To which class of organic compounds does each of the following compounds belong?

4. CH_3CH_2COOH

5. $CH_3CH_2CH_2OH$

6. $CH_3CH_2OCH_3$

7. CH_3COCH_3

Think of Questions 4–7 as multiple-choice questions with the answer choices listed before the questions. The questions have been rewritten as complete sentences.

4. To which class of organic compounds does CH_3CH_2COOH belong?

To identify the class of compound, you need to identify the functional group. The highlighted functional group in the formula is $-COOH$, which is a carboxyl group.

Which compounds contain a carboxyl group? That's right, carboxylic acids. Find the choice that matches this answer.

The correct answer is D.

5. To which class of organic compounds does $CH_3CH_2CH_2OH$ belong?

The highlighted functional group is $-OH$, a hydroxyl group. Alcohols contain hydroxyl groups. Find the choice that matches this answer.

The correct answer is A.

6. To which class of organic compounds does $CH_3CH_2OCH_3$ belong?

The functional group is $-O-$. Which group contains this functional group?

The correct answer is C.

Now you try it.

7. To which class of organic compounds does CH_3COCH_3 belong?

Hint: The functional group is $-CO$, a carbonyl group.

_____

Characterize the reactions in Questions 10–14 as an addition, esterification, oxidation, polymerization, or substitution reaction. You will be shown how to solve Questions 10–12. Then you will solve Questions 13 and 14 on your own.

10. $CH_3CHO \xrightarrow[H_2SO_4]{K_2Cr_2O_7} CH_3COOH$

Compare the formulas for the reactant and product. The product has one more oxygen atom. The product has gained oxygen.

The reaction is an oxidation reaction.

11. $CH_2 = CH_2 + HCl \longrightarrow CH_3CH_2Cl$

In this reaction, two reactants form one product. Hydrogen and chlorine are added to the double bond of the alkene. The product is an alkane.

The reaction is an addition reaction.

12. $CH_3CO_2H + CH_3CH_2OH \xrightarrow{H^+}$
$CH_3COOCH_2CH_3 + H_2O$

Identify the functional group in each reactant. One functional group is −COOH. The other functional group is −OH. So the reactants are a carboxylic acid and a alcohol.

The product is an ester. The reaction is an esterification reaction.

Now you try it.

13. $xCH_2 = CH_2 \longrightarrow H + CH_2 - CH_2 \xrightarrow{}_x H$

Hint: Note the coefficient x in front of the reactant.

The reaction is a(an) _____ reaction.

14.

Hint: What has been added to the benzene ring? What has been removed?

The reaction is a(an) _____ reaction.

24 Standardized Test Prep Tutor

Use the paragraph to answer Questions 8–10.

Because an amino acid contains a carboxyl group and an amino group, it is amphoteric; that is, it can act as either an acid or a base. Crystalline amino acids have some properties—relatively high melting points and high water solubilities—that are more characteristic of ionic substances than of molecular substances.

8. Write an equation showing glycine acting as an acid in a reaction with water. (Glycine is the simplest amino acid. Its side chain is R = H.)

9. Write an equation showing glycine acting as a base in a reaction with water.

10. It is possible for glycine to undergo an internal Brønsted-Lowry acid-base neutralization reaction. Write the resulting structural formula. Explain how this reaction would account for the ionic properties of glycine.

Focus on one question at a time. The key phrases have been highlighted.

8. Write an equation showing glycine acting as an acid in a reaction with water. (Glycine is the simplest amino acid. Its side chain is R = H.)

An amino acid has a central atom of carbon.

From the paragraph you know that an amino acid has an amino group, $-NH_2$, and a carboxyl group, $-COOH$. It also has a hydrogen atom, H, and a side group, R. In this case, the R group is H. Because you have 2 H atoms you can combine them as H_2. Write the molecular formula for glycine.

The molecular formula for glycine is _____.

Glycine is in a reaction with water. Set up your equation by writing the reactants.

_____ + _____ ⟶

Glycine can act as an acid by donating a proton during a reaction. The proton is a hydrogen ion from the carboxyl group. The hydrogen ion moves from the carboxyl group to the water molecule. Use this information to write the products of the reaction.

$NH_2CH_2COOH + H_2O \longrightarrow$
NH_2CH_2 _____ + _____

9. Write an equation showing glycine acting as a base in a reaction with water.

Now you're going to show how glycine can act as a base during a reaction in water. The reactants are the same as those in question 8. Write the reactants.

_____ + _____ ⟶

Glycine can act as a base by accepting a proton during a reaction. The proton is a hydrogen ion from the water. The amino group in glycine accepts this hydrogen ion. Use this information to write the products of the reaction.

$NH_2CH_2COOH + H_2O \longrightarrow$

$^+$_____CH_2COOH + _____

10. It is possible for glycine to undergo an internal Brønsted-Lowry acid-base neutralization reaction. Write the resulting structural formula. Explain how this reaction would account for the ionic properties of glycine.

The acid-base neutralization reaction is an internal reaction. That means the glycine molecule is both a proton donor and a proton acceptor.

In question 8, you found out that the carboxyl group in glycine donates a proton to act as an acid. In question 9, you found out that the amino group in glycine accepts a proton to act as a base. What happens when glycine acts as both an acid and a base during a reaction?

_____

_____

_____

_____

The molecular formula for glycine is NH_2CH_2COOH. This formula changes to $^+NH_3CH_2COO^-$ after the Brønsted-Lowry acid-base neutralization reaction. What is the structural formula for glycine after this internal reaction?

Glycine is a neutral molecule after the neutralization reaction. So why would it have ionic properties? Look at the molecular or structural formula of glycine to answer this question.

_____

_____

_____

_____

_____

Now you try it.

Write an equation showing alanine acting as an acid in a reaction with water. (Alanine is an amino acid with a side chain of R = CH_3. The molecular formula for alanine is $CH_3CH(NH_2)COOH$.)

_____

_____

Interpret Graphs
Ratio of Neutrons to Protons in Nuclei

Lesson 25.2

Preview the Graph

The graph shows the relationship between the number of neutrons and the number of protons in all known stable nuclei. A stable nucleus is one that does not decay.

Number of protons is on the *x*-axis. How does the number of protons change as you move from left to right across the graph?

_____

Number of neutrons is on the *y*-axis. What is the range of values for the *y*-axis?

_____

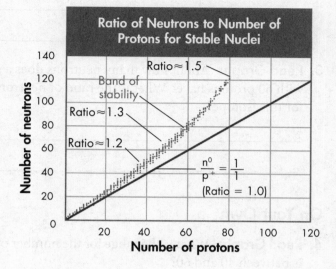

The black line shows the pattern you would see if every stable nuclei had a 1 to 1 ratio of neutrons to protons. The slope of the black line is constant.

Look at the region on the graph labeled "band of stability." Each blue dot in this region represents one of the 264 known stable nuclei. Look at the pattern formed by the dots. Does every stable nuclei have a 1 to 1 ratio of neutrons to protons? Explain.

_____

_____

Analyze the Graph

Now you are ready to answer some more questions. As you read the questions:

► Highlight key words.
► Circle numbers and units.

Use the first question as an example.

1. **Read Graphs** About how many neutrons does a stable isotope with ⟨20⟩ protons have? What is the ratio of neutrons to protons for this isotope?

_____

> **Try it!** Find 20 on the x-axis. Follow the vertical line to the band of stability. Find the value on the y-axis for this location.

2. Estimate Find the part of the band of stability that falls between 20 protons and 40 protons on the *x*-axis. What is the range for the number of neutrons in this part of the band of stability?

_____

_____

> **Try it!** Mark the bottom and top of the part of the band that falls between 20 and 40 on the *x*-axis. Draw lines from the marks to the *y*-axis and estimate the values.

3. Read Graphs About how many neutrons does a stable isotope with 60 protons have? What is the ratio of neutrons to protons for this isotope?

_____

_____

> **Try it!** Find 60 on the *x*-axis. Find the matching value on the *y*-axis. Divide the *y*-axis value by the *x*-axis value to find the ratio.

On Your Own

4. Read Graphs What is the range for the number of neutrons when the number of protons is between 40 and 60?

_____

_____

5. Read Graphs About how many neutrons does a stable isotope with 80 protons have? What is the ratio of neutrons to protons for this isotope?

_____

_____

_____

6. Make Generalizations What happens to the ratio of neutrons to protons in stable isotopes as the number of protons increases?

_____

_____

_____

7. Infer For what range of atomic numbers do stable nuclei exist? How do you know?

_____

_____

_____

Interpret Graphs Decay Curve

Lesson 25.2

Preview the Graph

Read the title of the graph. A decay curve shows what happens to a radioisotope over time. The variable on the *x*-axis is number of half-lives. What is the variable on the *y*-axis?

_____

_____

Look at the atomic windows. These drawings can help you picture what happens to an isotope as it decays. The blue dots represent atoms of reactant. The gray dots represent atoms of the decay product.

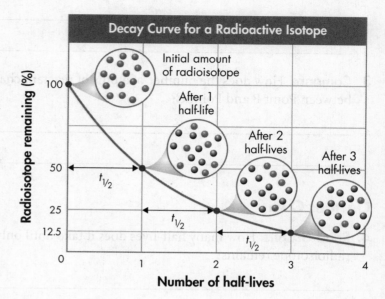

Look at the atomic window for Point A. There are 16 blue dots in the window. They represent the initial amount of radioisotope.

Look at the atomic window for Point B. Describe what you see.

_____

_____

Analyze the Graph

Now you are ready to answer some more questions. As you read the questions:

▶ Highlight key words.
▶ Circle numbers and units.

Use the first question as an example.

1. Read Graphs When the number of half-lives is 0, what percent of radioisotope remains?

_____

> **Try it!** Find 0 on the *x*-axis. Follow the vertical line to Point A. Find the value for this point on the *y*-axis.

2. Read Graphs At Point B, what are the values for number of half-lives and percent of radioisotope remaining?

_____

_____

> Try it! Find Point B. Follow the lines from the point to the x-axis and the y-axis.

3. Compare How does the number of atoms of reactant change between Point B and Point C?

_____

_____

> Try it! Find the atomic windows for Point B and Point C. Count the number of atoms of reactant in each window.

On Your Own

4. Read Graphs How many half-lives does it take until only 12.5 percent of the radioisotope remains?

_____

5. Compare How does the number of atoms of reactant change between Point C and Point D?

_____

6. Make Generalizations What happens to the percent of a radioisotope remaining during each half-life?

_____

7. Predict Use the percent of radioisotope remaining when the number of half-lives is 3 to predict the percent of radioisotope remaining when the number of half-lives is 4.

_____

_____

More Practice Using Half Lives

Step-by-Step Practice

1. Radon-222 emits alpha radiation. It has a half-life of 3.8 days. A radon-222 sample has an initial mass of 2.0×10^{-6} grams. How many grams of radon-222 remain after 11.5 days?

❶ Analyze List the knowns and the unknowns.

Knowns	Unknowns
$t_{1/2}$ = 3.8 days	number of half-lives = ?
initial mass = 2.0×10^{-6} g	mass remaining = ? g
decay time = 11.5 days	

❷ Calculate Solve for the unknown.

First, calculate the number of half-lives. Then divide the decay time by the half-life.

$$\text{Number of half-lives} = \frac{\text{number of days}}{\text{half-lives}}$$

$$\text{Number of half-lives} = \frac{11.5 \text{ days}}{3.8 \text{ days}} = 3.0 \text{ half-lives}$$

Multiply the initial mass by one half for each half-life. Write the answer in scientific notation with the correct number of significant figures.

$$\text{Remaining mass} = 2.0 \times 10^{-6} \text{ g} \times \frac{1}{2} \times \frac{1}{2} \times \frac{1}{2}$$

$$= 2.0 \times 10^{-6} \text{ g} \times \frac{1}{8}$$

$$= 0.25 \times 10^{-6} \text{ g} = 2.5 \times 10^{-7} \text{ g}$$

❸ Evaluate Does the result make sense?

Three half-lives have passed. So it makes sense that the initial mass has been reduced by one-eighth. Dividing the final mass by the initial mass gives the decimal equivalent of one-eighth (0.125).

....

2. The isotope technetium-99^{m} emits X-rays. It has a half-life of 361 minutes. How many grams of a 1.50×10^{-5} gram sample remain after a decay time of 1440 minutes?

❶ Analyze List the knowns and the unknowns.

Knowns	Unknowns
$t_{1/2}$ = 361 minutes	number of half-lives = ?
initial mass = _____	mass remaining = ? g
decay time = _____	

❷ **Calculate** Solve for the unknown.

Calculate the number of half-lives.

Half lives $= \dfrac{}{361 \text{ min}} = \underline{\hspace{2cm}}$

Then calculate the remaining mass.

Remaining mass $= \underline{\hspace{2cm}} \times \dfrac{1}{2} \times \dfrac{1}{2} \times \dfrac{1}{2} \times \dfrac{1}{2}$

$= \underline{\hspace{2cm}}$

❸ **Evaluate** Does the result make sense?

_____

_____

_____

On Your Own

3. The isotope, promethium-147, has a half-life of 2.62 years. How many grams of an initial 5.40 g sample will remain after 5.24 years?

4. Radium-228 decays by beta emission and has a half-life of 5.76 years. What mass of radium-228 in a 7.5 g sample will remain after 17.3 years?

5. Polonium-218 is a hazardous isotope because it emits high energy alpha particles. Its half-life is 182 seconds. How many milligrams of a 1.00 milligram sample of polonium-218 remain after 546.7 seconds?

25 Standardized Test Prep Tutor

Use the drawings of atomic nuclei to answer Question 9.

(A) 　(B) 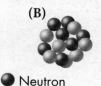　(C)

⬤ Proton　⬤ Neutron

You will be shown how to find the name and symbol for isotope A and isotope B. Then you will find the name and symbol for isotope C on your own.

9. Write the name and symbol for each isotope.

Start with isotope A. Count the number of protons and neutrons in the drawing. The element with six protons is carbon.

The atomic number of the isotope is equal to the number of protons. Add the number of protons and neutrons to find the mass number of the isotope.

Use this information to write the name and symbol for isotope A. In the symbol, the atomic number is the superscript. The mass number is the subscript.

Count the number of protons and neutrons in the drawing for isotope B. The element with seven protons is nitrogen.

Use this information to identify the atomic number and mass number of the isotope.

What is the name of isotope B? What is its symbol?

Now you try it.

What is the name of isotope C? What is its symbol?

Notes and Calculations

Number of protons: 6

Number of neutrons: 8

Atomic number: 6

Mass number: 14

Name: carbon-6

Symbol: $^{14}_{6}C$

Number of protons: 7

Number of neutrons: 7

Atomic number: 7

Mass number: 14

Name: nitrogen-14

Symbol: $^{14}_{7}N$

Name: _____

Symbol: _____

**Use the graph to answer Questions 11–13. You will be shown
how to solve Questions 11 and 12. Then you will solve
Question 13 on your own.**

Estimate the percent of the radioisotope that remains
after the given number of half-lives.

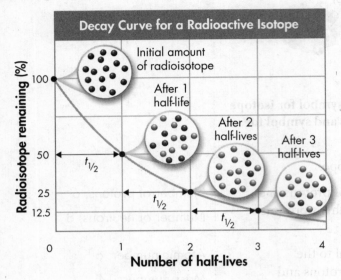

The questions have been rewritten as complete sentences.

11. Estimate the percent of the radioisotope that remains
after 0.5 $t_{1/2}$.

    The graph shows that half of the radioisotope, or 50 percent,
    remains after one half-life. You need to estimate what
    percent remains after less than one half-life.

    Find the point on the x-axis that is halfway between the
    0 and the 1. Use a pencil to draw a vertical line from
    that point to the decay curve. Then draw a horizontal
    line from the decay curve to the y-axis.

    About 70 percent of the
    radioisotope remains after
    0.5 $t_{1/2}$.

12. Estimate the percent of the radioisotope that remains after
1.25 $t_{1/2}$.

    After 1.25 half-lives, more than one half-life and less than
    two half-lives have passed.

    Find the point on the x-axis that is about 25 percent of the
    way between the 1 and the 2. Estimate the value on the
    y-axis that corresponds to this point.

    About _____ percent of the
    radioisotope remains after
    1.25 $t_{1/2}$.

    Now you try it.

13. Estimate the percent of the radioisotope that remains after
3.75 $t_{1/2}$. *Hint:* The point on the x-axis will be between
the 3 and the 4.

    About _____ percent of the
    radioisotope remains after
    3.75 $t_{1/2}$.